IN HIS LIKENESS

IN HIS LIKENESS

*Forty Selections on the Imitation of Christ
Through the Centuries*

BY G. McLEOD BRYAN

* * * * * * * * * * *

John Knox Press
RICHMOND, VIRGINIA

Library of Congress Catalog Card Number: 59-10455

✴ FOREWORD

G. McLeod Bryan has long made the theme of the imitation of Christ a particular object of interest and now makes available to fellow Christians this collection of great statements on the subject. The anthology calls to our attention how persistent through the centuries has been the effort not only to understand but also to live the Christian life as one of discipleship to Jesus, of walking in His steps, of imitating Him as pattern, of suffering Him to remake us in His image. Even men who prefer some other great phrase and idea to summarize what Christian life is at its core—"Doing the Will of God" or "Seeking the Vision of God" or "Being Citizens of the Kingdom or City of God"—must introduce this theme into their reflections; for Jesus Christ has done the will of the Father; in Him the vision of God has come to men; He is the pioneer of the Kingdom, the first citizen of the *Civitas Dei*.

So rich a collection of thoughts upon the theme calls attention to the many facets of the work of Christ on men—a work we try as vainly to summarize in our theological theories as we try to define His person in our Christologies. He comes into view as a worker in human history who does ever new things which cannot be adequately described in any of our conventional categories though we may pile them up and add to the offices of prophet, priest, and king such other activities as those of the teacher, the physician, the artist, the pioneer, the discoverer. What He is doing we know not now because its greatness transcends the grasp of those who can only know parts and in part. But we have the assurance that we shall understand hereafter.

We are reminded too by these many ways of Christ-following and Christ-imitation how various is the material on which He works; how much in consequence only He remains the center of the great community of His disciples; how little any members of groups in that community can set up the way Christ has molded their thought and action as a standard others must observe. No two followers of Christ can walk in His steps in exactly the same way. Some can run; some must follow on crutches; some stride forward with undiminished vigor; more of them in faltering weakness depend on the constant help of the One who though He walks before returns ever and again to pick up and encourage those fallen by the way. Some cannot follow faithfully except as they keep faith with families or nations for whom they bear responsibility; others cut themselves loose from all such ties and accept the word about leaving the dead to bury the dead as spoken directly to them. If we change the parable from "walking in His steps" to "imitation" the variety of Christian life still remains in view. There are those Jesus Christ calls upon to imitate Him as a child imitates a parent; those others whom He sets to work to copy His words and deeds; and still others who, like advanced apprentices, are being taught to be and to do an independent work that is in the spirit of the Master Workman.

There is always cause for rejoicing among Chistians that Christ their Master brings so great and varied a company of disciples together and leads them in such manifold ways. There is always also cause for the sober reflection that every discipleship remains an imitation and that only the original One is a fit Pattern, Example, and Master.

H. RICHARD NIEBUHR
New Haven, Connecticut

✳ CONTENTS

✳ INTRODUCTION:
The Challenge

"The Imitation of Christ is a subject which is constantly calling for reconsideration," said James Stalker. "Each generation sees it in its own way, and the last word on it can never be spoken." This anthology has as its purpose to show the fullness of the example of Christ for Christian ethical living and the many-sidedness of the motif as it expresses itself in devout Christians of twenty centuries.

Christians of every generation have explored the meaning of the imitation of Christ for daily living. Ignatius prayed in the first century, "Permit me to be an imitator of the passion of Christ, my God." *In His Steps* by Charles M. Sheldon is a modern attempt to apply to American culture the Jesus way of living. Indeed the essence of Christianity consists in the double feature of God's giving Himself in the redemptive act of Christ and of our growing in the likeness of Christ as we seek to follow Him in everyday living.

The heartbeat of Christianity is given in the classic invitation of Christ found in Matthew 11:28-29. The inflow is, "Come unto me . . . and I will give you rest . . ."; and the outflow is, "Take my yoke upon you, and learn of me . . ." The former is the redemptive element of the Cross in the incarnate Son of God, the latter is the responsive element of the Cross in us. Certainly the full Gospel, evangelical Christianity, has always insisted on both *sacramentum et exemplum*—Christ both the gift of grace and the perfect example of redeemed human nature.

Christianity has found in the imitation of Christ a broad common denominator where its many diverse strains unite: heretics and ecclesiastics, laymen and theologians, the Eastern and the Western Church, the practical man and the

13

suffering saint, the high churchman and the sectarians, the activists and the contemplators—even males and females. While its interpretations range all the way from mechanically copying certain minor particulars of Jesus' life to Luther's inclusive conception of "Being Christ to one's neighbor," it keeps close to the vital center of our faith. As we examine the variations upon this theme we shall touch Christianity at every level.

However, genuine imitation allows for creativity; it never imitates literally. What is desired are not imitations of Christ. Obviously, where the vocation of Jesus is regarded as unique, imitation is presumptuous. Nevertheless, in the positive, creative sense we are all called "to be conformed to the image of his Son."

Christians are cross-bearers; as such, they are imitators of the Lord. Dietrich Bonhoeffer warns: "There is always a danger that in our asceticism we shall be tempted to imitate the sufferings of Christ. This is a pious but godless ambition, for beneath it there always lurks the notion that it is possible for us to step into Christ's shoes and suffer as He did. We are then presuming to undertake that bitter work of eternal redemption which Christ Himself wrought for us."

This "anthology with comments" is compiled to share with Christians the thrill—yea, and the rebuke—of discovering the countless passages on the imitation of Christ in the writings of the renowned and the obscure in these twenty centuries of Christianity. The forty selections were finally chosen not alone for their contribution to the unfolding of the theme, but also because they express varied presentations of the theme. Sources are mentioned in every case in the hope that the taste given here will lead the reader to the full meal to be gained from reading the whole work. If these words stir your heart to a more complete commitment to the Crucified and Indwelling Lord, then this book will be more than an earthly blessing.

THE GOSPELS and THE EPISTLES: "Follow Me"

Unquestionably the writers of the Epistles conceived of Christianity as a way of life that entailed imitation of Jesus of Nazareth, both Christ and New Adam. (See 1 Corinthians 15:49.) This impression Christ had made upon His closest associates, both writers of the Gospels and writers of the Epistles. Paul commanded: "Be imitators of me, as I am of Christ" (1 Corinthians 11:1), and he commended the Thessalonians for becoming "imitators of us and of the Lord" (1 Thessalonians 1:6). John declared, "He who says he abides in him ought to walk in the same way in which he walked." (1 John 2:6.) And Peter affirmed, "For to this you have been called, because Christ also suffered for you, leaving you an example, that you should follow in his steps." (1 Peter 2:21.) The Letter to the Hebrews gave constant prominence to Christ as the new and absolute pattern: "Therefore, holy brethren, who share in a heavenly call, consider Jesus . . . Although he was a Son, he learned obedience through what he suffered; and being made perfect he became the source of eternal salvation to all who obey him." (Hebrews 3:1 and 5:8-9.) According to the emphasis of this book, Jesus blazed the trail, cut the absolute and authoritative pattern of the new creature. But, as Lindsay Dewar has reminded us, since "pattern" is used of inanimate and "likeness" of animate and personal beings, the latter term is to be preferred. The portrait that stands at the forefront of Christian history to which our lives are to be likened is the figure of the incarnate Christ Himself. To imitate God, to cultivate divine likeness, is not foreign to the Biblical ethics, nor is it original with the Judaeo-Christian position. What is new is that in Christ the divine

15

pattern is made comprehensible and concrete. C. H. Dodd says that "the imitation of Christ, being the imitation of God Himself so far as God can be a model to His creatures, becomes a mode of absolute ethics."

The foregoing references proclaim imitation in general, but there are many verses in the Epistles which specify a particular virtue manifest in Christ the model. *Love:* "And walk in love, as Christ loved us." (Ephesians 5:2.) *Humility:* "By this we know love, that he laid down his life for us; and we ought to lay down our lives for the brethren." (1 John 3:16.) *Purity:* "And every one who thus hopes in him purifies himself as he is pure." (1 John 3:3.) *Long-suffering:* "Since therefore Christ suffered in the flesh, arm yourselves with the same thought." (1 Peter 4:1.) *Forgiveness:* "As the Lord has forgiven you, so you also must forgive." (Colossians 3:13.) *Self-denial:* "Let each of us please his neighbor for his good, to edify him. For Christ did not please himself." (Romans 15:2-3.) Here imitation of Christ is quite simple: We observe the way Jesus behaved in certain situations and these provide the model for our behavior in similar situations. These become the newly revealed virtues of Christianity.

More often, though, the apostolic conception of imitation is in terms of conformity. Here imitation is not so much conscious reproduction of the externals as the inner, creative attitude of the Mind of Christ. Imitation is the inner man consorting with the Living Christ. Imitation results from spiritual meditation on the life of the incarnate Lord and what He has done for man. Paul was the great exponent of this conception with his axiom: "I have been crucified with Christ; it is no longer I who live, but Christ who lives in me." (Galatians 2:20.) His explanation of the Christian's relationship to Christ is a variation upon this theme: "For those whom he foreknew he also predestined to be conformed to the image of his Son, in order that he might be the firstborn among many brethren." (Romans 8:29.) "But put on the Lord Jesus Christ." (Romans 13:14.) "That I may know him and the power of his resurrection, and may share his sufferings, becoming like him in his death." (Philippians 3:10.)

Subsequent Christianity has not always known whether imitation should be literal, as some of the preceding references seem to imply, or in terms of the newly revealed spiritual virtues of Christ, or in terms of mystical conformity. But one thing is unavoidable: in the instruction of Jesus Himself, discipleship means to learn His way of life, and follow-ship means to take up the cross in His manner. The words, "Follow me" (Mark 1:17), were apparently the first to arrest the hearts of His hearers. Peter later claimed that he and the other disciples had undertaken just that: "Lo, we have left everything and followed you." (Mark 10:28.) Jesus countered with His stringent mandate that before one can say he is following, he must have "left house or brothers or sisters or mother or father or children or lands." (Mark 10:29.) The last words Jesus spoke to the disciples before His ascension were, according to the Gospel of John, "Follow me" (John 21:19); and the very last word was spoken to Peter, "Follow thou me." (John 21:22, K.J.V.) Thus, from the beginning to the end of the earthly ministry of Jesus, the indelible impression upon the minds of those most closely associated with the Master held that He intended discipleship in terms of follow-ship.

The way in which His disciples are to follow He clearly elaborated: "If any man would come after me, let him deny himself and take up his cross and follow me. For whoever would save his life will lose it; and whoever loses his life for my sake and the gospel's will save it." (Mark 8:34-35.) Luke inserted "daily." (Luke 9:23.) The counsel

Christ gave to the rich young ruler is well known: "If you would be perfect, go, sell what you possess and give to the poor, and you will have treasure in heaven; and come, follow me." (Matthew 19:21.) Again, in the Gospel of John, which emphasizes so much the way of life exemplified by Christ, our Lord declared: "If any one serves me, he must follow me; and where I am, there shall my servant be also." (John 12:26.) Thomas complained, as so many have confessed since, "Lord, we do not know where you are going; how can we know the way?" Jesus replied in no uncertain terms: "I am the way, and the truth, and the life; no one comes to the Father, but by me." (John 14:5-6.) The preceding saying, plus the two listed next, has been used most frequently by the Christ-imitators as their Biblical proof-texts. All three of these statements have been taken as applying to a way of life, rather than in the sense of specific counsel such as that offered to the rich young ruler. "Take my yoke upon you, and learn from me; for I am gentle and lowly in heart, and you will find rest for your souls." (Matthew 11:29.) "For I have given you an example, that you also should do as I have done to you." (John 13:15.)

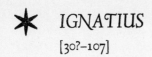

IGNATIUS

[30?–107]

"Only let me attain unto Jesus Christ," are the notable words by which this early martyr lived his discipleship. Ignatius is said to have cried with joy upon hearing his sentence prior to being taken to Rome where he was executed: "I thank Thee, O Lord, that Thou hast vouchsafed to honour me with a perfect love towards Thee, and hast made me to be bound with iron chains, like Thy Apostle Paul."

Being one of the Apostolic Fathers, what Ignatius had to say on imitation is all the more impressive when it is remembered that he was in point of time so close to the New Testament Church. His eye upon martyrdom, his willingness to bear the cross, his appreciation of suffering—these were all centered in his express desire to imitate the passion of Christ. He perceived the power of the Christian life to be fellowship with Christ in His maltreatment at the hands of sinful men. "From whom we also derive our being, from His divinely blessed passion, that He might set up a standard for the ages." In exhorting Christians he reminded them to "despise not the period of forty days [Lent?], for it comprises an imitation of the conduct of the Lord." His plea from the beginning to the end of his seven letters to various churches is: "Permit me to be an imitator of the passion of Christ, my God."

The imitation of Ignatius belongs to the extreme sort that became the "seed of the Church." He speaks of himself as "the wheat of God" and longs for the day when he shall be "ground by the teeth of wild beasts into the pure bread of Christ."

For now I begin to be a disciple, and I speak to you as my fellow-servants. For it was needful for me to have been admonished by you in faith, exhortation, patience, and long-suffering. But inasmuch as love suffers me not be silent in regard to you, I have therefore taken upon me first to exhort you that ye would run together in accordance with the will of God. For even Jesus Christ does all things according to the will of the Father . . . Wherefore it behoves us also to live according to the will of God in Christ, and to imitate Him as Paul did. For, says he, "Be ye followers of me, even as I also am of Christ.". . . Thus, being joined together in concord and harmonious love, of which Jesus Christ is the Captain and Guardian, do ye, man by man, become but one choir; so that, agreeing together in concord, and obtaining a perfect unity with God, ye may indeed be one in harmonious feeling with God the Father, and His beloved Son Jesus Christ our Lord. For, says He, "Grant unto them, Holy Father, that as I and Thou are one, they also may be one in us." It is therefore profitable that you, being joined together with God in an unblameable unity, should be the followers of the example of Christ, of whom also ye are members.

*   *   *   *   *   *

Do ye therefore, clothing yourselves with meekness, become the imitators of His sufferings, and of His love, wherewith He loved us when He gave Himself a ransom for us, that He might cleanse us by His blood from our old ungodliness, and bestow life on us when we were almost on the point of perishing through the depravity that was in us. Let no one of you, therefore, cherish any grudge against his neighbour.

* * * * * *

Now I begin to be a disciple, and have no desire after anything visible or invisible, that I may attain Jesus Christ. Let fire and the cross; let the crowds of wild beasts; let breakings, tearings, and separations of bones; let cutting off of members; let bruising to pieces of the whole body; and let the very torment of the devil come upon me: only let me attain to Jesus Christ . . .

* * * * * *

I long after the Lord, the Son of the true God and Father, even Jesus Christ. Him I seek, who died for us and rose again. Pardon me, brethren: do not hinder me in attaining to life; for Jesus is the life of believers. Do not wish to keep me in a state of death, for life without Christ is death. While I desire to belong to God, do not ye give me over to the world. Suffer me to obtain pure light: when I have gone thither, I shall indeed be a man of God. Permit me to be an imitator of the passion of Christ, my God.

* * * * * *

I endure all things for Christ . . . that I may suffer together with Him, while He Himself inwardly strengthens me.

CLEMENT *of* ALEXANDRIA

[c. 150–c. 220]

Clement, who became the headmaster of the catechetical school of Alexandria, "the second Athens," endeavored to relate the Christian good with Greek theory. His textbooks, largely ethical, are lengthy descriptions of the Christian life in terms of the "gnostic" response to the best in Jesus and Plato. Nonetheless, he conceived "salvation as the following of Christ." In the third work of his famous trilogy, he writes: "Striving, then, to attain to the summit of knowledge [*gnosis*]; decorous in character; composed in mien; possessing all those advantages which belong to the true Gnostic; fixing his eye on fair models, on the many patriarchs who have lived rightly, and on very many prophets and angels reckoned without number, and above all, on the Lord, who taught and showed it to be possible for him to attain that highest life of all,— he therefore loves . . . the things hoped for." The second book of the trilogy, *The Instructor*, pictures Christ the divine Logos become flesh, marking the way whereby all who follow Him shall do "greater works than these."

It is essential to note at this point that Eastern Christianity, particularly the later, more developed forms of Eastern Orthodoxy, continued to emphasize the imitation of Christ, though they turned from Clement to a more mystical interpretation. They stressed the imitation of Jesus Christ, the very God incarnate, in His humiliated status. Their Christology came to be known as the kenotic theory, a part of which pertains to the imitation of Christ in His *kenosis*, self-emptying, and it derives largely from Philippians 2:5-8. Certain Eastern and Russian Orthodox saints, especially Theodosius and Tychon, of a later period, were outstanding exponents of this view. In Nestor's *Life of Theodosius,* one reads: "Good Theodosius replied humbly: 'Listen to me. Our Lord Jesus Christ became poor and humbled Himself, offering Himself as an example, so that we should humble ourselves in His name.'" In Tychon's *Confession* are found these words: ". . . Set my feet upon the rock; and straighten my steps, so that I may follow you, my Liberator and my only Leader, guiding me to heaven and to eternal life. Draw me after You, O burning Love! Let me run in the path You have trod."

The Instructor

Having now accomplished those things, it were a fitting sequel that our instructor Jesus should draw for us the model of the true life, and train humanity in Christ.

Nor is the cast and character of the life He enjoins very formidable; nor is it made altogether easy by reason of His benignity. He enjoins His commands, and at the same time gives them such a character that they may be accomplished.

The view I take is, that He Himself formed man of the dust, and regenerated him by water; and made him grow by His Spirit; and trained him by His word to adoption and salvation, directing him by sacred precepts; in order that, transforming earth-born man into a holy and heavenly being by His advent, He might fulfil to the utmost that divine utterance, "Let Us make man in Our own image and likeness." And, in truth, Christ became the perfect realization of what God spake; and the rest of humanity is conceived as being created merely in His image.

But let us, O children of the good Father—nurslings of

the good Instructor—fulfil the Father's will, listen to the Word, and take on the impress of the truly saving life of our Saviour; and meditating on the heavenly mode of life according to which we have been deified, let us anoint ourselves with the perennial immortal bloom of gladness—that ointment of sweet fragrance—having a clear example of immortality in the walk and conversation of the Lord; and following the footsteps of God, to whom alone it belongs to consider, and whose care it is to see to, the way and manner in which the life of men may be made more healthy.

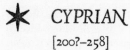 CYPRIAN

[200?–258]

Cyprian's treatise, "On Patience," is described by the Catholic historian Felix Vernet as "the most touching invitation to imitate Jesus in Christian antiquity." Perhaps he was able to write so movingly because, like his Master, he gave up so much and suffered almost continually, until he was finally martyred during the first universal persecution of Christians begun by the Emperor Decius.

Cyprian turned to Christ late in life and apparently forsook position in order to follow the Humble Saviour. Throughout the remainder of his days, even when he became bishop, he understood Christianity in terms of imitation: "But he follows Christ who stands in His precepts, who walks in the way of His teaching, who follows His footsteps and His ways, who imitates that which Christ both did and taught; in accordance with what Peter also exhorts and warns, saying, 'Christ suffered for us, leaving you an example, that ye should follow His steps.'"

For the many *lapsii*—those Christians who saved their lives by momentarily paying respects to Caesar in emperor worship, thereby inviting excommunication from the Church for idolatry—Cyprian pled charitableness, citing the example of Jesus Christ's doing as much in seeking the one lost sheep. A churchman of the first order, Cyprian appealed throughout his numerous treatises to the example of Christ on behalf of tolerance and humility.

25

But for us, beloved brethren, who are philosophers, not in words, but in deeds, and do not put forward our wisdom in our garb, but in truth—who are better acquainted with the consciousness, than with the boast, of virtues—who do not speak great things, but live them,—let us, as servants and worshippers of God, show, in our spiritual obedience, the patience which we learn from heavenly teachings. For we have this virtue in common with God. From Him patience begins; from Him its glory and its dignity take their rise. The origin and greatness of patience proceed from God as its author. . . .

And that we may more fully understand, beloved brethren, that patience is a thing of God, and that whoever is gentle, and patient, and meek, is an imitator of God the Father; when the Lord in His Gospel was giving precepts for salvation, and, bringing forth divine warnings, was instructing His disciples to perfection, He laid it down, and said, "Ye have heard that it is said, Thou shalt love thy neighbour, and have thine enemy in hatred. But I say unto you, Love your enemies, and pray for them which persecute you; that ye may be the children of your Father which is in heaven, who maketh His sun to rise on the good and on the evil, and raineth upon the just and on the unjust. For if ye love them which love you, what reward shall ye have? do not even the publicans the same? And if ye shall salute your brethren only, what do ye more (than others)? do not even the heathens the same thing? Be ye therefore perfect, even as your Father in heaven is perfect." He said that the children of God would thus become perfect. He showed that they were thus completed, and taught that they were restored by a heavenly birth, if the patience of God our Father dwell in us—if the divine likeness, which Adam had lost by sin, be manifested and shine in our actions. What a glory is it to become like to God! what and how great a felicity, to possess among our virtues, that which may be placed on the level of divine praises!

Nor, beloved brethren, did Jesus Christ, our God and Lord, teach this in words only; but He fulfilled it also in deeds. And because He had said that He had come down for this purpose, that He might do the will of His Father; among the other marvels of His virtues, whereby He showed forth the marks of a divine majesty, He also maintained the patience of His Father in the constancy of His endurance. Finally, all His actions, even from His very advent, are characterized by patience as their associate; in that, first of all, coming down from that heavenly sublimity to earthly things, the Son of God did not scorn to put on the flesh of man, and although He Himself was not a sinner, to bear the sins of others. His immortality being in the meantime laid aside, He suffers Himself to become mortal, so that the guiltless may be put to death for the salvation of the guilty. The Lord is baptized by the servant; and He who is about to bestow remission of sins, does not Himself disdain to wash His body in the laver of regeneration. For forty days He fasts, by whom others are feasted. He is hungry, and suffers famine, that they who had been in hunger of the word and of grace may be satisfied with heavenly bread. He wrestles with the devil tempting Him; and, content only to have overcome the enemy, He strives no further than by words. He ruled over His disciples not as servants in the power of a master; but, kind and gentle, He loved them with a brotherly love. He deigned even to wash the apostles' feet, that since the Lord is such among His servants, He might teach, by His example, what a fellow-servant ought to be among his peers and equals. . . .

But if we also, beloved brethren, are in Christ; if we put Him on, if He is the way of our salvation, who follow Christ in the footsteps of salvation, let us walk by the example of

Christ, as the Apostle John instructs us, saying, "He who
saith he abideth in Christ, ought himself also to walk even
as He walked." Peter also, upon whom by the Lord's condescension the Church was founded, lays it down in his
epistle, and says, "Christ suffered for us, leaving you an
example, that ye should follow His steps, who did no sin,
neither was deceit found in His mouth; who, when He was
reviled, reviled not again; when He suffered, threatened not,
but gave Himself up to him that judged Him unjustly."

Finally, we find that both patriarchs and prophets, and all
the righteous men who in their preceding likeness wore the
figure of Christ, in the praise of their virtues were watchful
over nothing more than that they should preserve patience
with a strong and stedfast equanimity.

*   *   *   *   *   *

The virtue of patience is widely manifest, and its fertility
and liberality proceed indeed from a source of one name, but
are diffused by overflowing streams through many ways of
glory; nor can anything in our actions avail for the perfection
of praise, unless from this it receives the substance of its
perfection. It is patience which both commends and keeps
us to God. It is patience, too, which assuages anger, which
bridles the tongue, governs the mind, guards peace, rules
discipline, breaks the force of lust, represses the violence of
pride, extinguishes the fire of enmity, checks the power of
the rich, soothes the want of the poor, protects a blessed
integrity in virgins, a careful purity in widows, in those who
are united and married a single affection. It makes men humble in prosperity, brave in adversity, gentle towards wrongs
and contempts. It teaches us quickly to pardon those who
wrong us; and if you yourself do wrong, to entreat long and
earnestly. It resists temptations, suffers persecutions, perfects
passions and martyrdoms. . . . It is this which directs our

doing, that we may hold fast the way of Christ while we walk by His patience. It is this that makes us to persevere as sons of God, while we imitate our Father's patience.

✳ LACTANTIUS

[c. 260–c. 340]

Sometimes called the Christian Cicero, Lactantius undertook the ambitious task of instructing the pagan emperor in *The Divine Institutes*, or "Introduction to True Religion." He aimed to present Christianity's rational side to the educated class. While the work encompasses the whole of theology, it is primarily concerned with ethics. Lactantius recognized Jesus' role as Mediator and Priest of a new religion, but he emphasized His role as Teacher and Exemplar of righteousness. Book IV, entitled "Of True Wisdom and Religion," stresses this note: "And since Christ came upon earth, supplied with virtue and righteousness, yea rather, since He Himself is virtue, and Himself righteousness, He descended that He might teach it and mould the character of man." He endeavored to associate the Greek concept of justice with the kind of moral life exemplified by Jesus Christ. He conceived of Christ as the best example of both. Christ came not to transform the nature of man by abstractly uniting it with the nature of God, but to teach virtue and exhibit it. Thus he interpreted the Incarnation: "Therefore, when God had determined to send to men a teacher of righteousness, He commanded Him to be born again a second time in the flesh, and to be made in the likeness of man himself, to whom He was about to be a guide, and companion, and teacher." His traits deserving emulation are humiliation, frailty, and suffering.

Few writers have appealed to the philosophic mind as persuasively as the apologist Lactantius in the following account.

If any one gives to men precepts for living, and moulds the characters of others, I ask whether he is bound himself to practise the things which he enjoins, or is not bound. If he shall not do so, his precepts are annulled. For if the things which are enjoined are good, if they place the life of men in the best condition, the instructor ought not to separate himself from the number and assemblage of men among whom he acts; and he ought himself to live in the same manner in which he teaches that men ought to live, lest, by living in another way, he himself should disparage his own precepts, and makes his instruction of less value, if in reality he should relax the obligations of that which he endeavours to establish by his words. For every one, when he hears another giving precepts, is unwilling that the necessity of obeying should be imposed upon him, as though the right of liberty were taken from him. Therefore he answers his teacher in this manner: I am not able to do the things which you command, for they are impossible. For . . . you forbid me to be excited by desire, you forbid me to fear pain or death; but this is so contrary to nature, that all animals are subject to these affections. Or if you are so entirely of opinion that it is possible to resist nature, do you yourself practise the things which you enjoin, that I may know that they are possible? But since you yourself do not practise them, what arrogance is it, to wish to impose upon a free man laws which you yourself do not obey! You who teach, first learn; and before you correct the character of others, correct your own. . . .

Whence it comes to pass, that no one obeys the precepts of the philosophers. For men prefer examples rather than words, because it is easy to speak, but difficult to accomplish.

Would to heaven that there were as many who acted well as there are who speak well! But they who give precepts, without carrying them out into action, are distrusted; and if they shall be men, will be despised as inconsistent: if it shall be God, He will be met with the excuse of the frailty of man's nature. It remains that words should be confirmed by deeds, which the philosophers are unable to do. . . . For no one since the creation of the world has been such, except Christ, who both delivered wisdom by His word, and confirmed His teaching by presenting virtue to the eyes of men. . . .

What will that teacher of righteousness say in reply to these things? How will he refute and convict a man who shall allege the frailty of the flesh as an excuse for his faults, unless he himself also shall be clothed with flesh, so that he may show that even the flesh is capable of virtue? For obstinacy cannot be refuted except by example. For the things which you teach cannot have any weight unless you shall be the first to practise them; because the nature of men is inclined to faults, and wishes to sin not only with indulgence, but also with a reasonable plea. . . .

Therefore, that a teacher may be perfect, no objection ought to be brought forward by him who is to be taught, so that if he should happen to say, You enjoin impossibilities; the teacher may answer, See, I myself do them. But I am clothed with flesh, and it is the property of flesh to sin. I too bear the same flesh, and yet sin does not bear rule in me. It is difficult for me to despise riches, because otherwise I am unable to live in this body. See, I too have a body, and yet I contend against every desire. I am not able to bear pain or death for righteousness, because I am frail. See, pain and death have power over me also; and I overcome those very things which you fear, that I may make you victorious over pain and death. I go before you through those things which you allege that it is impossible to endure: if you are not able to follow me giving directions, follow me going before you. In this way all excuse is taken away, and you must confess that man is unjust through his own fault, since he does not follow a teacher of virtue, who is at the same time a guide. You see, therefore, how much more perfect is a teacher who is mortal, because he is able to be a guide to one who is mortal, than one who is immortal, for he is unable to teach patient endurance who is not subject to passions. . . .

Let men therefore learn and understand why the Most High God, when He sent His ambassador and messenger to instruct mortals with the precepts of His righteousness, willed that He should be clothed with mortal flesh, and be afflicted with torture, and be sentenced to death. For since there was no righteousness on earth, He sent a teacher, as it were a living law, to found a new name and temple, that by His words and example He might spread throughout the earth a true and holy worship.

* * * * * *

For God (as I have before explained), when He had determined to set man free, sent as His ambassador to the earth a teacher of virtue, who might both by salutary precepts train men to innocence, and by works and deeds before their eyes might open the way of righteousness, by walking in which, and following his teacher, man might attain to eternal life. He therefore assumed a body, and was clothed in a garment of flesh, that He might hold out to man, for whose instruction He had come, examples of virtue and incitements to its practise. But when He had afforded an example of righteousness in all the duties of life, in order that He might teach man also the patient endurance of pain and contempt of death, by which virtue is rendered perfect and complete, He came into the hands of an impious nation, when, by the knowledge of the future which He had, He might have avoided them, and by the same power by which He did wonderful works He might have repelled them. Therefore He endured tortures, and stripes, and thorns. At last He did not refuse even to undergo death, that under His guidance man might triumph over death, subdued and bound in chains with all its terrors. But the reason why the Most High Father chose that kind of death in preference to others, with which He should permit Him to be visited, is this. For some one may perchance say: Why, if He was God, and chose to die, did He not at least suffer by some honourable kind of death? . . . why by an infamous kind of punishment, which may appear unworthy even of a man if he is free, although guilty? First of all, because He, who had come in humility that He might bring assistance to the humble and men of low degree, and might hold out to all the hope of safety, was to suffer by that kind of punishment by which the humble and low usually suffer, that there might be no one at all who might not be able to imitate Him.

BASIL the GREAT

[c. 330–379]

Monasticism from the beginning cited the example of
Christ as the absolute pattern for the regulation of Christian
conduct. Those who responded to Christ's counsel, "If thou
wouldst be perfect," went beyond the practices and devotions
of the ordinary lay Christian. From the time of St. Anthony
onward the three renunciations of the religious—of the World
(manifested by the vow of poverty), the Flesh (by chastity),
and Self-will (by obedience)—were drawn from the Gospel
account of the Master's life. Basil voiced monastical senti-
ment: "So he who is seized by the vehement desire of following Christ can no longer care for anything to do with this
life." The renunciations of the monk, in the likeness of his
Lord, he felt to be "the beginning of our being made like unto
Christ." The opening lines of *An Ascetic Discourse* by Basil
read: "For he that has imitated in his own life, so far as is
possible, the passionless character of the divine nature has
restored the image of God."

Nevertheless, he more than the usual advocate of monasticism saw imitation carrying a wider implication: "This is
the goal of Christianity, the imitation of Christ in the
measure of His humanity as far as the vocation of each man
permits." He became the reformer of monastic life, sub-
stituting constructive work and common life together for
that of hermitical asceticism. His comprehensive view allowed
for a more social-minded imitation: "The fashion of the
love of Christ does not allow us to look each at his own good.
. . . Now the solitary life has one aim, the service of the
needs of the individual."

The value of meditation upon the human life of Christ, so

35

important for later times, is indicated in the first passage, from *The Longer Rules* (XLIII); the second passage is from *The Morals*.

First of all then—which truly comes first—humility must be so practised by him in the love of Christ that even when he is silent the example of his deeds may stand out more strongly than any word as a means of teaching. For if this is the standard of Christianity, the imitation of Christ according to the measure of His Incarnation as is appropriate to the calling of each, those who are entrusted with the guidance of the many ought by their own mediation to lead on the weaker to the imitation of Christ, as the blessed Paul says: "Be ye imitators of me, as I am of Christ."

So they should first make themselves an accurate model by observing the standard of humility handed down by our Lord Jesus Christ. For "learn of me" He says "for I am meek and lowly of heart."

*   *   *   *   *   *

What is the mark of a Christian? To be cleansed from all pollution of flesh and spirit, in the blood of Christ . . .

What is the mark of those who eat the bread and drink the cup of the Lord? To keep in perpetual memory Him Who died for us and rose again.

What is the mark of those that keep such a memory? To live unto themselves no longer, but into Him Who died for them and rose again.

What is the mark of a Christian? That his righteousness should abound in everything, more than that of the Scribes and Pharisees, according to the measure of the teaching of the Lord in the Gospel.

What is the mark of a Christian? To love one another, even as Christ also loved us.

What is the mark of a Christian? To see the Lord always before him.

What is the mark of a Christian? To watch each night and day and in the perfection of pleasing God to be ready, knowing that the Lord cometh at an hour he thinketh not.

AUGUSTINE *of* HIPPO
[354–430]

"God is our journey's end, and Man-Christ, our way to it," might well be taken as the motto of Augustine. He held that the way of the world is *superbia*, prideful self-sufficiency; that the way of the Eternal City is *humilitatis*, loving interdependence. Besides redeeming His own, Christ set the pattern for their citizenship in the Eternal City: "Let us not therefore look for a more easy way; by the road on which He preceded us, let us also go; let us follow by the road on which He has led. . . . On this cross, indeed, throughout the whole of this life which is spent in the midst of trials and temptations, the Christian must continually hang."

Christ is both gift and example, *sacramentum et exemplum*: "He built for Himself here below a lowly house of our clay, that by it He might bring down from themselves and bring up to Himself those who were to be made subject, healing the swollenness of their pride and fostering their love: so that their self-confidence might grow no further but rather diminish, seeing the deity at their feet, humbled by the assumption of our coat of human nature: to the end that weary at last they might cast themselves down upon His humanity and rise again in its rising."

Christ the Representative Man, *verus-homo*, displayed a new type of love wrought through suffering and humility: "Why art thou proud, O man? God for thee became low. Thou wouldst perhaps be ashamed to imitate a lowly man; then at least imitate the lowly God." The famous passage on the humility revealed in Christ is contained in Book VII of his *Confessions*, the theme of which is "that by His example men might learn humility."

Christ, the perfect man, Augustine regarded primarily as an authoritative exemplar of the mystic way to the beatific vision. "The first is wholly carried out here until the end of this world, but in the world to come it hath no end. . . . Let perfect action *follow me*, informed by the ensample of My Passion: but let contemplation that has been begun, *tarry till I come*, to be perfect when I come." Thus borrowing heavily from his Platonic training, Augustine set the stage for medieval mysticism with its goal of *unio mystica*, union with the Godhead, toward which imitation of Christ is but a means. From the beginning to the end of his thought, the theme is "through the Man-Christ to the God-Christ."

Now, they are wanting in wisdom who pose this question: "Why could not God in His wisdom have found a way to liberate men other than by assuming man's nature, being born of a woman and suffering all those injuries at the hands of sinners?" To these we reply: Most assuredly, God could have devised another plan; but, if He had acted otherwise, He would incur your stupid displeasure just the same. For, if He had not come into bodily view of sinners, they would not be able to behold with their unclean minds His eternal Light, which is seen by the eyes of the soul.

But, now that He has deigned to remind us by His visible presence to prepare for things unseen, He is a source of displeasure to the greedy, because He did not have a body made of gold; a source of displeasure to the impure, because He was born of a woman (for the unchaste detest the fact that women conceive and beget children); a source of displeasure to the proud, because He bore insults with perfect patience; a source of displeasure to lovers of ease, because He suffered torments; a source of displeasure to the faint-hearted, because He suffered death. To remove the impression that they are defending their own vices, they say that these points displease them, not as found in man, but as found in the Son of God. They do not understand the meaning of God's eternity that has assumed a human nature; they do not have a grasp of human nature itself, which by a change within itself was restored to original soundness. We may thus learn from the Lord's teaching that the infirmities we have contracted by sinning can be healed by right living.

*   *   *   *   *   *

Let the human race take hope and rediscover its own nature. Let it see what an important place it occupies among the works of God. Men! do not despise yourselves—the Son of God assumed manhood. Women! do not despise yourselves —the Son of God was born of a woman. Yet, do not love things carnal, for in the sight of the Son of God we are neither male nor female. Do not love things temporal; for, if it were right to love them, the human nature assumed by the Son of God would have loved them. Do not be afraid of insults and crosses and death, for, if these were harmful to man, the human nature assumed by the Son of God would not have suffered them.

This entire exhortation, which is now everywhere preached, everywhere reverently received, restoring health to docile souls, would have no place in human affairs, had not those events occurred which are a source of displeasure to the unwise. For example, what can bring a perverse pride to the practice of virtue, if it is ashamed to imitate Him of whom it was said before His birth: "He shall be called the Son of the Most High." And it is an undeniable fact that He is now called the Son of the Most High throughout all nations. If we have a high opinion of ourselves, let us deign to imitate

Him who is called the Son of the Most High. If we have a lowly opinion of ourselves, let us presume to imitate the fishermen and publicans who imitated Him.

O Medicine, making provision for all: deflating what is distended; renewing what is wasting away; cutting away what is superfluous; preserving what is necessary; restoring what has been lost; curing what is corrupted! Who will now raise himself up against the Son of God? Who can despair of his own salvation, for whom the Son of God has willed to become so lowly? Who can believe that happiness is to be found in those things which the Son of God has taught us to despise? What tribulation can overcome him who believes that in the Son of God human nature was preserved intact amid violent persecution? Who can imagine himself shut out from the kingdom of heaven when he knows that publicans and prostitutes have imitated the Son of God? What wickedness can be found in him who makes that Man's deeds and words the object of his contemplation, love, and striving, in whom the Son of God revealed Himself to us as a pattern of life?

✳ GREGORY the GREAT

[c. 540–604]

"Every preacher should give forth a sound more by his deeds than by his words, and rather by good living imprint footsteps for men to follow than by speaking show them the way to walk in." No one was more qualified to offer this advice than Gregory the Great, whose experience in administration as pope and whose conception of the work of Christ were both intensely practical. Most of his writings, as the one quoted from above, *The Book of Pastoral Rule*, gave detailed instructions for Christian morality. His *Dialogues*, which have been described as "rules for good living," and his *Moralia*, comments upon the book of Job, were equally practical.

For this emphasis Gregory has been accused of Pelagianism —the doctrine that the saving power of Jesus Christ inheres in His peerless example which inspires correspondent likeness. Certainly such a saying as the following could evoke such a charge: "Christ might have redeemed us even without dying; His death was only to show us the greatness of the love of God." However, anyone who is at all acquainted with the remainder of his beliefs, especially that related to the divinity of Christ, could hardly make the charge. The probable explanation is that Gregory's emphasis upon ethics led him to conceive the significance of Christ's redemption as lying in the example which He has given us. "All that which our blessed Saviour wrought in His mortal body, He did it for our example and instruction, to the end that, following His steps, according to our poor ability, we might without offence pass over this present life."

In the English edition of *Moralia* the page headings for

42

the following excerpt bespeak well his position: "Footsteps of the Christ-God the Saints' Rule of Life."

And so we, when we behold the efficacy of His long-suffering and pitifulness, and upon so beholding strive to imitate the same, what else do we but follow the 'footsteps of His goings,' in that we imitate some outskirts of His method of proceeding. Thus these footsteps of His Father 'Truth' gave it in charge to imitate when He said, *Pray for them which persecute you and falsely accuse you; that ye may be the children of your Father Which is in heaven. For He maketh His sun to rise on the evil and on the good.* It may be too that blessed Job who had already said with assured faith, *I know that my Redeemer liveth, and that I shall arise at the latter day from the earth;* so dwelt on the future working of Wisdom Incarnate to be, in like manner as we behold by faith the works of that Wisdom now past, how that the Mediator between God and man should be kind to give, humble to bear, patient to afford an example. Whose life while blessed Job, filled with the Spirit from above, regarded with heedful intentness, foreseeing the future lowliness of His mild character, he refers as it were to a pattern set before him, so that whatever he did in this life he might bind fast to His footsteps in imitating, that so he who was incapable of seeing the high things of His secret ordering, as it were looking on the ground, might keep His footsteps for imitation. Of which same 'footsteps' of Him it is said by Peter, *Because Christ also suffered for us, leaving us an example, that ye should follow His footsteps.*

*   *   *   *   *   *

But who is there represented by the name of 'balances,' saving the Mediator between God and man? In Whom all our merits are weighed with an even scale, and in Whose precepts we find what we have come short in our own life. Now we are weighed in these balances as often as we are incited after the examples of His life. Thus it is hence that it is written; *Christ also suffered for us, leaving you an example, that ye should follow His steps, Who did no sin, neither was guile found in His mouth; Who when He was reviled, reviled not again, when He suffered, He threatened not.* Hence it is said by Paul, *Let us run with patience the race that is set before us: looking unto Jesus, the Author and Finisher of our faith, Who for the glory set before Him endured the Cross, despising the shame.* Accordingly to this end the Lord appeared in the flesh, that the life of man He might by dealing admonitions arouse, by giving examples kindle, by suffering death redeem, by rising again renew.

* * * * * *

For He was therefore made a Man amongst us, not only to redeem us by the shedding of His blood, but also to change us by setting an example. He found therefore one thing in our conversation at His coming, and taught us another by His life. For all the progeny of the haughty race of Adam were striving to seek after the prosperity of the present life, to avoid its adversities, to escape disgrace, to follow glory. The Incarnate Lord came amongst them courting adversity, scorning prosperity, embracing insults, flying from glory. For when the Jews had wished to make Him their king, He shrunk from being a king. But when they were endeavouring to kill Him, He came of His own accord to the scaffold of the cross. He therefore avoided that which all seek after, He sought after that which all avoid; He caused all to marvel that both He Himself rose again when dead, and by His death raised others from death. For there are in truth, two lives of a man who exists in the body, one before death, the other after the resurrection; one of which all practically knew, but knew not the other; and mankind were directing their thoughts to that only which they knew. The Lord came in the flesh, and while He took on Himself the one, He pointed out the other. While He took on Himself that which was known to us, He pointed out to us that which was unknown to us. For by His dying He practised that life which we possess, by rising again He disclosed that life for which we are to seek, instructing us by His example, that this life which we pass before our death, is not to be loved on its own account, but to be tolerated on account of the other. Because then, by practising a new conversation amongst men, He followed not the customs of Babylon, it is well written of Him, *He scorneth the multitude of the city.*

* * * * * *

He set forth in Himself patterns of both lives, that is, the active and the contemplative, united together. For the contemplative life differs very much from the active. But our Redeemer by coming Incarnate, while He gave a pattern of both, united both in Himself. For when He wrought miracles in the city, and yet continued all night in prayer on the mountain, He gave His faithful ones an example, not to neglect, through love of contemplation, the care of their neighbours, nor again to abandon contemplative pursuits, from being too immoderately engaged in the care of their neighbours; but so to keep together their mind, in applying it to the two cases, that the love of their neighbour might not interfere with the love of God, nor again the love of God cast out, because it transcends, the love of their neighbour.

BERNARD of CLAIRVAUX
[1090–1153]

Hymns attributed to Bernard, including "O Sacred Head Now Wounded" and "Jesus, Thou Joy of Loving Hearts," typify his Christo-centric mysticism.

"Historically," writes A. C. McGiffert, "even more important than Bernard's emphasis on the divine Christ and mystical union with Him, was his emphasis on the human Christ and his constant insistence that the Christian life lies in imitating Him." Bernard with all his interests, mystical and monastic, was a preacher who never wearied of offering Jesus to the awakening masses as the loving example. "In vain," he wrote, "are we called Christians, if we live not according to the example and discipline of Christ, the Father of the institution."

With the Bernadine mysticism Jesus returns to the center of devotion. Until then the flighty thought of Dionysian mysticism, with its abstract talk of the flight of the alone-with-the-Alone, had held sway; Bernard and his followers returned to Augustinian piety and its attention to the humanity of Christ. Certainly there is in Bernard much emotional verbalism and a tendency toward idle contemplation, but his contribution is that meditation on the life of Christ moves us to imitate that life. As Bernard would say, His wisdom teaches us and His love moves us; but it is His humility which above all we must imitate.

He insisted that in the traits of humility and love the imitation principally consists. He forever preached imitation of Christ. The theme of the Song of Songs, his text for the following sermons, is the excellencies of Jesus in answer to the perennial query of the Greek mind: "Sir, we would see Jesus."

So let the Lord tell us of the toil of the way and of the reward of that toil. He says, "I am the way, the truth, and the life." He calls humility the way which leads to truth. The former is toil; the latter, the fruit of the toil. How am I to know, you ask, that He was speaking of humility when He said simply, "I am the way"? But hear this, which is clearer: "Learn of me, for I am meek and lowly in heart." He offers Himself as an example of humility, as the type of gentleness. If you follow Him, you shall not walk in darkness, but shall have the light of life.

* * * * * *

It is thus, then, that Thy Beloved, leaving all things for Thy sake, desires to follow after Thee, to walk closely in Thy footsteps always, and to follow Thee whithersoever Thou goest, knowing that Thy ways are ways of blessedness, and all Thy paths are peace, and that therefore he who followeth Thee walks not in darkness.

* * * * * *

I am the Rose of Sharon and the Lily of the valleys. She then points to the couch; but He summons her to the plain —that is, He excites her to vigorous effort. He regards it as the most persuasive argument possible to her to enter upon this struggle that He should propose Himself to her either as an example for one engaged in the struggle, or a reward for one that has overcome in it. The words may be understood in either of these two senses. Thou, O Lord Jesus, art to me both a mirror of endurance and the reward of enduring. The one is a powerful incentive; the other a great encouragement. By the example of Thy valour Thou dost teach my hands to war; by the Presence of Thy Majesty Thou dost crown me after the victory.

* * * * * *

A book or writing has no single point of goodness for me if I do not read therein the Name of Jesus; nor has a conference any interest for me, unless the Name of Jesus be heard in it. As honey to the mouth, as melody in the ear, as a song of gladness to the heart, is the Name of Jesus. But it is also a medicine. Is any of you sad? Let Jesus come into your heart; let His Name leap thence to your lips, and behold, when that blessed Name arises [as a sun], its light disperses the clouds of sadness, and brings back serenity and peace. . . .

Nothing is so powerful as the Name of Jesus to restrain the impulse of anger, to repress the swelling of pride, to cure the wound of envy, to bridle the impulse of luxury, and extinguish the flame of fleshly desire; to temper avarice, and put to flight ignoble and impure thoughts. For, when I utter the Name of Jesus, I set before my mind, not only a Man meek and humble in heart, moderate, pure, benign, merciful, and, in short, conspicuous of every honourable and saintly quality, but also in the same individual the Almighty God, who both restores me to spiritual health by His example, and renders me strong by His assistance. . . . Of His example I make, as it were, medicinal and salutary herbs, and His help is an instrument to prepare them . . .

* * * * * *

These conciliate on my behalf the Judge of all the world, showing to me Him who is so greatly to be feared, as one who is gentle and humble, and not only making Him willing to receive and to pardon, but even more, in giving me Him who is far above all powers, and terrible among the kings of the earth, as a model for me to imitate. It is for these reasons that I have these [sufferings of Jesus] frequently in my mouth, as you know, and always in my heart, as God knows. These are familiar themes in all my writings, as is well known. In a word, my philosophy is this, and it is the loftiest in the world: to know JESUS, and Him crucified. . . . For if you have Him whom you are bearing, always before your eyes, it is certain that, beholding the pains and troubles which the Lord endured, you will more easily and willingly bear your own, by His help.

✸ FRANCIS of ASSISI

[1182–1226]

St. Francis is acclaimed by the world as the nearest imitator of Christ. Bartholomew's biography, *Conformity of the Life of Blessed Francis with the Life of the Lord Jesus*, legendary though some of it may be, holds that Francis in every action of his life imitated Christ, and that the famous stigmata came from heaven as a divine attestation of this. In this account forty resemblances between Christ and Francis are mentioned. If this be the case, it was no more than the fulfillment of Francis' life purpose. "Naked, he would follow the naked Christ," was his manner of living the Gospel pattern; and in answer to the Voice from the cross, saying thrice, "Francis, go and repair My House, which, as thou seest, is falling utterly into ruin," he endeavored to challenge the Church to return to its primitive purity. That state he conceived to be the following of Christ in His poverty and His identification with common things. He would be a doer of the Word: "For it becomes us by the example of Christ rather to do than to teach." He insisted that the "brethren be called Minors for this reason, that they should not presume to become greater. For their vocation teaches to remain lowly, and to imitate the footsteps of the humility of Christ." Moreover, he "was unwilling that his friars should be desirous of knowledge and books, but he willed and preached to them that they should desire to be founded on holy humility, and to imitate pure simplicity, holy prayer, and our Lady Poverty, on which the saints and first friars did build. And this, he used to say, was the only safe way to one's salvation and the edification of others, since Christ, to Whose imitation we are called, showed and taught us this alone by word and example alike."

50

Even his famous love for natural life, the birds and flowers, was rooted in his respect for "Him who is called the 'flower of the field' and 'the lily of the valley.'" He insisted on imitation to the last: "Wishing in his death to imitate his Lord and Master, as he had perfectly imitated Him in his life, he ordered loaves to be brought to him, and blessed them, and made them to be broken into portions . . ."

One trait uniquely Franciscan, though, was the joy he manifested throughout at the very privilege of being called to imitate Christ.

See, Lord Jesus, Poverty is to that extent the Queen of the Virtues that you left the haunts of the angels and came down on earth so you could betroth her to you in everlasting love and beget all the children of perfection in Poverty, and of it, and through it. And Poverty clung to you so faithfully that she began her service to you in the very womb of your Mother, where you had of all living bodies the tiniest. Then too as you came forth from the womb, she welcomed you to the holy manger and the stable, and as you went about in the world, she kept you so despoiled of everything that she had you do without a place to rest your head.

But also she went with you faithfully as your most loyal companion when you undertook the battle for our redemption. In the very clash of your suffering she was there as your inseparable armor-bearer, and though the disciples deserted you and denied knowing you, she did not abandon you but stayed faithfully at your side with all the company of her noble peers. Yes when, because the cross was so high, your very Mother—and such a Mother!—could not reach you (though she cherished you faithfully even then and remained

in union with your sufferings with anguished affection)—
then, I say, Lady Poverty was there like a most welcome
handmaiden with all her privations to enfold you more tightly
than ever and to share them more feelingly in your torment.

*   *   *   *   *   *

Oh, who would not love this your Lady Poverty above all
others! I entreat you for the favor of being sealed with this
privilege, I crave to be enriched with this treasure. I beg you,
O Jesus most poor, that it may be the distinction of me and
mine forevermore, for your name's sake to possess nothing
under heaven as our own and to be sustained as long as our
poor flesh lives only with the closely restricted use of things
given us by others.

*   *   *   *   *   *

O Lord Jesus Christ, I entreat you to give me two graces
before I die: first, that in my lifetime I may feel in body and
soul as far as possible the pain you endured, dear Lord, in
the hour of your most bitter suffering; and second, that I may
feel in my heart as far as possible that excess of love by which
you, O Son of God, were inflamed to undertake so cruel a
suffering for us sinners.

*   *   *   *   *   *

The rule and life of these brothers is this, that they live in
obedience, in chastity, and without property, and follow the
teaching and the footsteps of our Lord Jesus Christ, who says:
"If you wish to be perfect, go and sell everything you have
and give it to the poor, and you shall have treasure in Heaven,
and come, follow me" (Mt. 19:21); and, "If anybody wishes
to come after me, let him deny himself and carry his cross
and follow me" (Mt. 16:24); likewise, "If anybody wishes
to come to me and he does not hate his father and mother and

wife and children and brothers and sisters, yes his very life, he cannot be my disciple" (Lk. 14:26).

*   *   *   *   *   *

All the brothers should try to follow the humility and poverty of our Lord Jesus Christ, and should mind that we ought not have anything else of all this world except that, as the apostle says, "having food and clothing enough, we be content with these" (1 Tim. 6:8). And they should be glad at associating with people of low rank and estimation, the poor and the feeble, the sick and the lepers, and people begging at the wayside.

And should it be necessary, let them go out for alms. And they should not be ashamed of it, but mind rather that our Lord Jesus Christ, the Son of the almighty living God, "set his face like a very hard rock" (Is. 50:7), and was not ashamed and was poor and shelterless and lived on alms.

*   *   *   *   *   *

Let us, brothers all, take note that our Lord says, "Love your enemies and do good to those who hate you" (Mt. 5:44). For also our Lord Jesus Christ, whose footsteps we should follow (I Pet. 2:21), called his betrayer friend and offered himself voluntarily to his crucifiers. All therefore who unjustly put on us trial and distress, shame and insult, grief and pain of various kinds together with martyrdom and death, are our friends, whom we ought to love much, because through what they put on us we obtain life everlasting.

✳ THOMAS AQUINAS

[1225–1274]

Part III of the *Summa Theologica*, "On the Incarnation," has been described by the Catholic historian Vernet as providing us "in so luminous a form a meditated Life of Christ." For anyone who knows the close-knit reasoning of the *Summa*, the discovery of a lyrical section is a delight. Vernet summarizes this section: "It is the Divinity of Christ which by right should move us most to love, and consequently to devotion, but that in fact it is rather the Humanity of Christ that touches our sensible nature, and the Humanity is 'the way which leads us to God.' Hence the Third Part is entitled: 'Of God made Man in order to lead us to God.' "

All in all, the *imitatio Christi* theme plays a minor part in Thomistic theology; but where it does appear, it incorporates both *sacramentum et exemplum* and the conception of the two levels of the religious life reflecting the consensus of the Middle Ages. Instances of the formula pertaining to the work of Christ appear in his answers to several questions. For example, to the question, "Whether it was becoming that Christ should be tempted?" he answers, "In order to give us an example: to teach us, to wit, how to overcome the temptations of the devil." Or, "Christ wished to make His Godhead known through His human nature. And therefore, since it is proper to man to do so, He associated with men, at the same time manifesting His Godhead to all, by preaching and working miracles, and by leading among men a blameless and righteous life." Or, again, "Christ's action is our instruction. In His manner of living our Lord gave us an example of perfection as to all those things which of themselves relate to salvation."

54

The two levels of the Christian life, "the religious" following more completely the counsels and example of Christ, are argued not only in a separate section of the *Summa* (Part II) but also in a special treatise Aquinas wrote, entitled "The Perfection of the Spiritual Life." The following excerpts from the *Summa* parallel his lines in that work.

Religious perfection consists chiefly in the imitation of Christ, according to Matt. 19. 21, *If thou wilt be perfect*, etc. . . . *follow Me*. Now in Christ obedience is commended above all according to Philip. 2.8, *He became* (Vulg.,—*becoming*) *obedient unto death*. Therefore it seems that obedience belongs to religious perfection.

* * * * * *

Our Lord declared that it belongs to the perfection of life that a man follow Him, not anyhow, but in such a way as not to turn back. Therefore He says again (Luke 9. 62): *No man putting his hand to the plough, and looking back, is fit for the kingdom of God*. And though some of His disciples went back, yet when our Lord asked (John 6. 68, 69), *Will you also go away?* Peter answered for the others: *Lord, to whom shall we go?* Hence Augustine says (*De Consensu Ev.* ii, 17) that "as Matthew and Mark relate, Peter and Andrew followed Him after drawing their boats on to the beach, not as though they purposed to return, but as following Him at His command." Now this unwavering following of Christ is made fast by a vow, and therefore a vow is requisite for religious perfection.

* * * * * *

Whether It Is Right to Say That Religious Perfection Consists in These Three Vows?

I answer that, The religious state may be considered in three ways. First, as being a practice of tending to the perfection of charity; secondly, as quieting the human mind from outward solicitude, according to I Cor. 7. 32: *I would have you to be without solicitude;* thirdly, as a holocaust whereby a man offers himself and his possessions wholly to God. And in corresponding manner the religious state is constituted by these three vows.

First, as regards the practice of perfection, a man is required to remove from himself whatever may hinder his affections from tending wholly to God, for it is in this that the perfection of charity consists. Such hindrances are of three kinds. First, the attachment to external goods, which is removed by the vow of poverty; secondly, the concupiscence of sensible pleasures, chief among which are sexual pleasures, and these are removed by the vow of continence; thirdly, the want of order in the human will, and this is removed by the vow of obedience.

In like manner the disquiet of worldly solicitude is aroused in man in reference especially to three things. First, as regards the dispensing of external things, and this solicitude is removed from man by the vow of poverty; secondly, as regards the control of wife and children, which is cut away by the vow of continence; thirdly, as regards the disposal of one's own actions, which is eliminated by the vow of obedience, whereby a man commits himself to the disposal of another.

Again, a holocaust is the offering to God of all that one has, according to Gregory (*Hom. viii in Ezech.*). Now man has a threefold good, according to the Philosopher. First, the good of external things, which he wholly offers to God by the vow of voluntary poverty; secondly, the good of his own body, and this good he offers to God especially by the vow of continence, whereby he renounces the greatest bodily pleasures; the third is the good of the soul, which man wholly offers to God by the vow of obedience, whereby he offers God his own will by which he makes use of all the powers and habits of the soul.

Therefore the religious state is fittingly constituted by the three vows.

*   *   *   *   *   *

Question XL, Article 1. Of Christ's Manner of Life

Reply Obj. 1. Christ wished to make His Godhead known through His human nature. And therefore, since it is proper to man to do so, He associated with men, at the same time manifesting His Godhead to all, by preaching and working miracles, and by leading among men a blameless and righteous life.

Reply Obj. 2. As stated in the Second Part, the contemplative life is, absolutely speaking, more perfect than the active life, because the latter is taken up with bodily actions: yet that form of active life in which a man, by preaching and teaching, delivers to others the fruits of his contemplation, is more perfect than the life that stops at contemplation, because such a life is built on an abundance of contemplation, and consequently such was the life chosen by Christ.

Reply Obj. 3. Christ's action is our instruction. And therefore, in order to teach preachers that they ought not to be forever before the public, our Lord withdrew Himself sometimes from the crowd. We are told of three reasons for His doing this. First, for the rest of the body: hence (Mark vi. 31) it is stated that our Lord said to His disciples:

"Come apart into a desert place, and rest a little. For there were many coming and going: and they had not so much as time to eat." But sometimes it was for the sake of prayer; thus it is written (Luke vi. 12): "It came to pass in those days, that He went out into a mountain to pray; and He passed the whole night in the prayer of God." On this Ambrose remarks that "by His example He instructs us in the precepts of virtue." And sometimes He did so in order to teach us to avoid the favour of men. Wherefore Chrysostom, commenting on Matth. v.1, Jesus, "seeing the multitude, went up into a mountain," says: "By sitting not in the city and in the market-place, but on a mountain and in a place of solitude, He taught us to do nothing for show, and to withdraw from the crowd, especially when we have to discourse of needful things."

* * * * * *

Question XL, Article 2. Of Christ's Manner of Life

Reply Obj. 1. In His manner of living our Lord gave an example of perfection as to all those things which of themselves relate to salvation. Now abstinence in eating and drinking does not of itself relate to salvation, according to Rom. xiv. 17: "The kingdom of God is not meat and drink." And Augustine explains Matth. xi.19, "Wisdom is justified by her children," saying that this is because the holy apostles "understood that the kingdom of God does not consist in eating and drinking, but in suffering indigence with equanimity," for they are neither uplifted by affluence, nor distressed by want. Again he says that in all such things "it is not making use of them, but the wantonness of the user, that is sinful." Now both these lives are lawful and praiseworthy—namely, that a man withdraw from the society of other men and observe abstinence; and that he associate with other men and live like them. And therefore our Lord wished to give men an example of either kind of life.

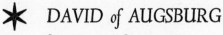

✳ DAVID of AUGSBURG

[c. 1200–1272]

Here again, in this first-generation Franciscan, we find that medieval Catholic allegiance to the Following, or rather to the Imitation of Christ, which the historian Luthardt claims, "forms the centre of the medieval state of mind down to the close of the Middle Ages." David of Augsburg had an unpublished manuscript called *Jesus Our Model*. He held that imitation of Christ is a special remedy for pride: "He who is inclined to fancy himself somewhat will begin to see himself, by contrast with Our Lord, as vile indeed, both in the spheres of well-doing and of endurance: he is as a locust to a giant, a pebble to a mount, a drop of water to a river." He continued in the vein Luther took later: "It shames us to imitate Our Lord in His humility and poverty, in His life of service and obedience, in His contumely, confusion, and contempt. Yet he who blushes to confess God before men or to imitate Him is not worthy of Him. It is great glory to follow the Lord." David's piety is thoroughly Bible-based, and he sought for the roots of Christianity. He definitely sided with those who believed the vocation to contemplative prayer not confined to the religious state, but possible in every walk of life. As we discover in these excerpts from his two-volume work *Spiritual Life and Progress*, he considered imitation of Christ to be the fountain of Christianity and formulated the classic evangelical balance, related so closely to the concept of corporate imitation given in the fourth chapter of the Epistle to the Ephesians.

In all this matter of holiness keep always before your mind, as a mirror and perfect example, the life and teaching of the Son of God, Our Lord Jesus Christ. For this He came, to open out before us the path of sanctity. His example sets for us a rule of life, He Himself instructs us that—created as we are to His *image*—we may be following His footsteps, renew in ourselves that *likeness* to Him which sin has defaced. Our nearness to Christ in heaven, our glory and splendour there, will be in proportion to the conformity we have achieved here between our life and His. Fix, then, your thoughts upon the words and ways of Jesus:

How humble He was with all, how gentle with His disciples, how modest in eating and drinking:

How kind He was to the poor, He made Himself as one of them, and they seemed especially His:

He scorned none, He shrank from none, not even the lepers:

He never flattered the rich; He was untrammelled by worldly cares, unanxious about temporal needs.

How chaste He was in His looks, how patient under insult, how mild in His answers.

He never strove, in biting, bitter words, to vindicate Himself, but sought to heal the malice of others by replying to them gently and humbly.

What burning zeal for the salvation of souls lay behind His quiet manner;

How lovingly He deigned to live and die for them.

So He stands before us, an example of all that is good. He shunned familiar intercourse with women, so that the disciples were astonished when they found Him—unlike His

usual custom—speaking alone with the Samaritan woman
(John iv, 27). He was patient under toil and privation,
full of sympathy for the afflicted, condescending to the
weakness of others, so upright that no adverse witness could
find aught against Him: He did not spurn sinners, and the
repentent He welcomed with clemency. In His words He
was equable, in prayer ardent and unremitting, and ever
ready to help: *I am in the midst of you as he that serveth*
(Luke xxii, 27). Remember His night-long vigils, His obedience to His parents, the entire absence in His life of any
boasting or ostentation; rather did He shun all the pomp
and glory of this world.

These and many other such characteristics of Our Lord's
life should be often in your mind so that in all you say
and do, walking, standing, sitting, eating, speaking or silent,
alone or in company, you may turn as to a guide to Him.
Thus you will come to love Him more, to draw near to
Him and become more familiar with Him; and He will become more real to you.

This, then, is the wisdom wherewith to store your mind.
Try to have constantly before you some thought or other
about Our Lord which will help you to imitate or to love
Him. Your time at meditation will be well spent if you are
occupied in thinking about Our Lord for you will at the
same time be moulding your own character in accord with
His life and teaching. Keep His example before you; and, in
every circumstance that presents itself, think how He would
have acted, and there you have at once the most perfect of
all models.

* * * * * *

Now just as no one could carry the entire tabernacle
single-handed [Num. 3-10], so no one can hope to model
his life perfectly on that of Our Lord. Our Lord did not

receive the spirit *in measure* (cf. John iii, 34), the spirit, that is, of holiness and of wisdom, but He received it in its entire *fulness* (cf. Col. ii, 9). Now of that *fulness* (cf. John i, 16), we all may take our share *according to the measure of the giving of Christ* (Eph. iv, 7), *one after this manner and another after that* (I Cor. vii, 7), one imitating Our Lord in this way, another in that, *until we all meet, in Heaven, unto a perfect man, unto the measure of the age of the fulness of Christ* (Eph. iv, 13), where everyone will find his place in the heavenly mansion, a place determined by the merit his zeal in imitating Our Lord has won for him.

✳ MEISTER ECKHART
[1260?–1327]

Right at the moment when the Church was amassing power and possessions to itself and when theology congealed in the famous *Summa Theologica* of Aquinas, there arose within the Church a movement which put primacy upon the soul's union with God through mystical fellowship. The "humanity of Christ" emphasis in Bernard, Francis, and Bonaventura took on even fresher significance in the ferment of northern Europe. Here in Germany, writes Luthardt, "it was not a dying world, but a humanity entering into history, with which Christianity had to deal. But this humanity required education and renewal. With this requirement the example of the man Jesus Christ comes into the foreground." Johannes Eckhart with his stress upon a more personal relationship to Christ and upon the application of Christianity to everyday life fathered a stream of thought which greatly influenced Luther two hundred years later. Those who associated themselves with this thought were known as Friends of God.

At a time when, "in place of the Gospel, we have adopted the decrees of the Pope; in place of Jesus, a certain Aristotle; in place of piety, ceremonies; and in place of truth, falsehood,"—as one of them pointedly confessed—they returned to the Scriptures, to Christ, and to simple brotherhood. One of Luther's letters credited them with "beginning the Gospel among you [the Germans]." Certainly the line from Eckhart through Tauler, Suso, Ruysbroeck, and Groote is clear. However, it may be said that Eckhart's approach was slightly more intellectual and closer to the contemporary Schoolmen in its analogy between the exemplary nature of

64

Christ and the Platonic ideas. Therefore, for Eckhart, the soul is imitation of God; Christ is exemplary of the soul in perfect harmony with God.

The tolerance indicated in these passages is typical of the mood which characterized the Christ-imitators from the very beginning, through the Inquisition of the Middle Ages, down to the modern conscientious objector.

Pious folk should imitate the deified man Christ. By imitating Christ I mean becoming Godlike. What I mean by Godlike is, your words, deeds, conduct, being free from human want. By human I mean imperfect.

* * * * * *

Now as to the strenuous life of imitation. Mark how it applies to thee. . . . for people are by no means all called upon to follow the same route to God, as St. Paul points out. . . . We ought to pay far more respect to other people's methods and despise no one's way. But let each one stick to his own way and, bringing all the other ways into line with that, profit in his own way by the merits of them all. . . . What you get in one way may be got in any other provided it is sound and good. . . .

Thou wilt say, "Our Lord Jesus Christ always took the highest way, we ought by rights always to follow him."—True, our Lord should be followed, generally speaking, but not in every detail. Our Lord fasted forty days: no one is called upon to copy him in that. Many things Christ did meaning us to copy the spirit not the letter; we must try to follow him intelligently, for he sets more store by what we think than by what we do. We have always got to follow him in the proper way.—"What way?"—How and in what way has to be decided in each case. . . . So a man can quite well follow our Lord by way of his own weakness, and need not, must not, think him far away.

*   *   *   *   *   *

I say that next to God there is no nobler thing than suffering. Were there anything more noble than suffering the heavenly Father would have given it to his Son Jesus Christ, in exemplary fashion, for all things. . . . I say, moreover, that had Christ been a man upon this earth without his deity, yet would he have been noble beyond all human ken by reason of his suffering; for granting that suffering is noble, he who has most suffering is the noblest. But no human suffering was equal to Christ's passion. And he is the more noble in proportion to it. Again I hold, if anything were nobler than suffering, God would have saved mankind therewith . . . Nothing is like suffering for killing a man's vices. Ergo, it makes a man Godlike. . . . Suffering alone is sufficient preparation for God's dwelling in man's heart.

*   *   *   *   *   *

Here let us examine the doctrine of virtue. Good life is in three ways a matter of will and primarily of resigning the will to God, for it is imperative to live up to one's lights, be it in taking or leaving. There are three kinds of will. The first is sensible will, the second is rational will, the third is eternal will. The sensible will needs guidance, proper teaching. The second is rational will: following in the footsteps of Christ Jesus and the saints, words, deeds and way of life all directed towards the highest end. Given this much God will give something more in the ground of the soul, to wit, eternal will and the amiable counsels of the

Holy Ghost. Says the soul, "Lord tell me, what is thy eternal will?" and then if she has satisfied the above conditions and if God so please, the Father will speak his eternal Word into the soul.

*   *   *   *   *   *

I once said that virgins follow the lamb wherever it goes, close behind. Some are virgins, some are not, whatever they appear. Wherever this lamb goes the virgins follow, some only while it leads them in the pleasant places that they like. When it takes them into suffering, travail and discomfort they turn back and refuse to follow, and these are not virgins for all they seem to be. Some say, Lord, I want to go in honour, riches, comfort. Well, if the lamb has led you by that way I wish you well in following his footsteps. True virgins will follow the lamb through the highways and the byways, whithersoever it may lead, and have no pity on themselves, befall what may.

✸ RICHARD ROLLE

[1290?–1349]

This St. Francis of English Christianity, like his spiritual counterpart on the continent, recalled the Church to its true mission—the love and service of Christ. By disposition a poet and a musician, his religious love lyrics in the vernacular prepared the ground for the reformation ferment in England: Langland, Chaucer, and Wyclif followed in his train.

Known primarily as a mystic, Rolle stood rather for experimental religion as distinct from the institutional and theoretical. As a Christian mystic, personal devotion to Christ was predominant in his life and teaching. Describing the stages of the mystic life in terms of *heat, song*, and *sweetness* in *The Fire of Love*, he repeatedly insisted that "the love of Christ must burn in us." This became the theme of his life, and though he was a recluse, his message burnt its way through the vanity of the religious and social structure of his day. From the time he was nineteen, home from his studies at Oxford and borrowing his sister's tunic to symbolize his acceptance of the simple life of Jesus, he became a wandering hermit, living truth and exposing sham. "Alas, for shame! An old wife is more expert in God's love, and less in worldly pleasure, than the great divine, whose study is vain. For why? For vanity he studies, that he may appear glorious."

Wherever he wandered—preaching, praying, serving, writing, singing—many were blessed. He gave light to those in spiritual darkness and a helpful hand and loving heart to those suffering mental and physical illness. He died apparently a victim of the Black Death, giving his life in saving others; for he was serving the nuns in a Cistercian convent during the epidemic.

Of the two writings quoted, both of which so aptly portray his spirit, the poem on the Passion is merely ascribed to him; it nonetheless calls attention to his firm belief that in "transcribing the suffering Christ" is life.

Of the Virtues of the Holy Name of Jesus

I went about, covetous of riches, and I found not Jesus. I ran in wantonness of the flesh, and I found not Jesus. I sat in companies of worldly mirth, and I found not Jesus. In all these I sought Jesus, but I found Him not. For He let me know by His grace that He is not found in the land of softly living. Therefore I turned another way, and I ran about in poverty, and I found Jesus, poorly born into the world, laid in a crib and lapped in cloths. I wandered in the suffering of weariness, and I found Jesus weary in the way, tormented with hunger, thirst and cold, filled with reproofs and blame. I sat by myself alone, fleeing the vanities of the world, and I found Jesus in the desert, fasting on the mountain, praying alone. I went the way of pain and penance, and I found Jesus bound, scourged, given gall to drink, nailed to the Cross, hanging on the Cross, and dying on the Cross.

*   *   *   *   *   *

THE EXAMPLE OF THE PASSION
"See what our Lord suffered for our sake"

Both young and old, where'er ye be,
   In Jesu's name good cheer ye make!
And lift ye up your hearts and see
   What our Lord suffered for our sake.

And meek as any Lamb was he,
  Ensample of him may we take,
To suffer too in our degree
  And in his service aye to wake.

And if our friends forsake us here,
  So that we be all alone,
Think we on Christ that bought us dear,
  And to him make all our moan:
 For of that Lord well may we learn
  What wrong he suffered am his foen;
When his disciples fled for fear,
  There 'bode no more but Mary and John.

If any wrong to us be wrought,
  Be it in word or else in deed,
Be of good cheer yet at the thought
  How God may help us all at need:
Think we how Jesus Christ us bought,
  And for our sins his blood did bleed;
For his own sinning was it not,
  For he did never sinful deed.

If wicked men do us defame,
  Think we how Christ was bought and sold;
For him to suffer is no shame,
  But him to serve look we be bold.
And if men injure our good name,
  We must forgive, both young and old;
For though we suffer so much blame
  Christ suffered more a thousandfold.

Of poverty if we complain,
  For that we lack some worldly good;
Think we on Jesu the Lord Sov'reign,
  How poor he hung upon the rood:

And how he strivèd not again,
　　But ever was meek and mild of mood;
To follow that Lord we should be fain,
　　In what degree that e'er we stood.

And though we have sorrow on each side,
　　And all about us wrong and woe,
Yet suffer meekly, and abide
　　And think on Christ that suffered also;
And how he was in full great dread,
　　Unto his pains when he should go:
He suffered more in his man-head
　　Than ever did man or ever shall do.

Though we with wrong to death be brought,
　　Yet suffering is the surest way;
For love of Jesu that us dear bought,
　　And died for us on Good-Friday;
So think we therefore in our thought
　　That we our Lord should please and pay,
And learn to set this world at nought,
　　And suffer wicked men to say.

In Jesu Christ was meekness most;
　　And therefore he the mastery had,
And bound the fiend for all his boast,
　　That never was he so sore a-dread;
Against his will and all his host
　　Adam and Eve with him he led,
And many more from out that coast
　　That were in prison full hard bestead.

If thou in Jesu have delight
　　Though all the world do thee assail,
Do after this; and thou shalt wit
　　Though meekness will thee most avail:

For whoso suff'reth here despite,
　And meekly abideth in that battail,
It will turn them to great profit,
　And endless joy for their travail.

If any do to us amiss,
　Or us in any wise offend,
For love of Jesu have mind on this,
　And let meekness thy mood amend
With Jesu Christ, as one of his,
　And suffer meekly what God shall send;
Then shall we be with him in bliss
　That aye shall last withouten end. Amen.

*　　*　　*　　*　　*　　*

. . . Take heed busily how thou followest Christ in manners. *Discite, inquit, a me quia mitis sum, et humilis corde.* "Learn of me," he says, "for I am meek and lowly of heart." He says not, "Learn of me for I am poor." Truly by itself poverty is no virtue but rather wretchedness; nor for itself praised, but because it is the instrument of virtue and helps to get blessedness, and makes many eschew many occasions of sinning. And therefore it is to be praised and desired. It lets a man from being honored, although he be virtuous; but rather it makes him despised and over led, and cast out among lovers of the world. To suffer all which for Christ is highly needful.

Therefore Christ to our example led a poor life in this way, for he knew that for them that abound in riches and liking it is hard to enter into heaven.

 HENRY SUSO

[c. 1300–1366]

For Suso, the German mysticism to which he attached himself, forming along with Eckhart and Tauler the "Friends of God," was an intimate personal adventure in the sufferings of our Saviour which gives life to the inner man. For eight years he bore on his bare back a cross pierced with nails "to make the sufferings of Christ more sensible." His life purpose, given in his autobiography, was "to learn to suffer like Christ." By this he meant that a Christian or "a meek man must be *deformed* from the creature, *conformed* to Christ, and *transformed* into the Deity." In his maxims he advised "how this and that friend of God first of all exercised themselves in imitating Christ's life and sufferings." The pattern Christ set entails the renunciation of worldly pleasures, the willingness to endure afflictions, and the "sweet doctrine, the gentle walk, and spotless life of our Saviour." Few passages of spiritual autobiography are as moving as the accompanying excerpts in which he described in the third person his own following.

He thought of suffering-imitation in a twofold sense. Comparing Christians to knights, he wrote: "Wherefore let not the faithful knights of a royal Master be discouraged; let us who follow in the steps of so noble a Leader take courage and suffer willingly; for if suffering brought us no other advantage, no further benefit, than to resemble that clear shining Mirror which is Christ, it would suffice." But, according to him, it does bring us another advantage: it enables the Christian soul to free itself "from the weight of sin, and soar upwards in the might of God into its divinely

73

illuminated reason, where it enjoys a perpetual influx of heavenly consolations."

In sharp contrast with the reality of his own imitation, he recorded unwittingly an account of the ever-present mockery of cross-bearing: "A holy maiden, who, when she perceived that her spiritual father was so devout to, and had such firm faith in, the loving Name of Jesus, which he bore upon his breast over his heart, conceived a great and peculiar love for it, and out of devotion she marked the Name of Jesus in red silk on a little piece of cloth, in the following form: IHS—and wore it secretly upon herself!"

PROLOGUE

The following book speaks throughout in an instructive manner of the life of a beginner, and contains, for those who look beneath the surface, information respecting the proper way in which a beginner should order his outer and inner man so as to be in harmony with God's all-lovely will. And since good works are undoubtedly a better guide, and sometimes shed a brighter light into a man's heart than mere words, therefore the book recounts, as examples, many different holy actions, which really and truly took place just as they are related. The book also tells of a man's progress in holiness; that is, how, by avoiding things, by sufferings, and by exercises, he may break through his unmortified animal nature, and arrive at great and exalted dignity.

*   *   *   *   *   *

In this fervour of devotion, he threw back his scapular, and, baring his breast, took in his hand a style; then, looking at his heart, he said:—Ah, mighty God! give me to-day strength and power to accomplish my desire; for Thou must be burnt to-day into my very inmost heart. Thereupon he set to work, and thrust the style into the flesh above his heart, drawing it backwards and forwards, up and down, until he had inscribed the Name of Jesus upon his heart. The blood flowed plenteously out of his flesh from the sharp stabs, and ran down over his body into his bosom; but this was so ravishing a sight to him through the ardour of his love, that he cared little for the pain. When he had finished, he went thus torn and bleeding from his cell to the pulpit under the crucifix, and kneeling down said:— Ah, Lord! my heart and soul's only love! look now upon my heart's intense desire. Lord, I cannot imprint Thee any deeper in myself; but do Thou, O Lord, I beseech Thee, complete the work, and imprint Thyself deep down into my very inmost heart, and so inscribe Thy holy Name in me, that Thou mayest never more depart from my heart.

Thus he bore upon him for a long time love's wound, until at length it healed up; but the Name of Jesus remained upon his heart, as he had wished, and the letters were about the breadth of a smooth stalk of corn, and the length of a joint of the little finger. In this way he bore the Name upon his heart until his death, and at every beat of his heart the Name moved with it.

* * * * * *

At first for a long time the Servitor [Suso himself] was, as it were, spoiled by God with heavenly consolations; and he was so eager after them, that all subjects of contemplation which had reference to the Divine nature were a delight to him; whereas, when he should have meditated upon our Lord's sufferings, and sought to imitate Him in them, this seemed to him a thing hard and bitter. He was once

severely rebuked by God for this, and it was said to him:—
Knowest thou not that I am the door through which all
true friends of God must press in, if they would attain to
true bliss? Thou must break thy way through My suffering
Humanity, if thou wouldst verily and indeed arrive at My
naked Divinity. The Servitor was struck with consternation
at this, and it was a hard saying to him; nevertheless . . . he
gave himself up to practise it with detachment.

* * * * * *

Above all his other exercises, he had a longing desire to
bear upon his body something which might betoken a
sensible sympathy with the painful sufferings of his crucified Lord. To this end he made for himself a wooden cross,
in length about a man's span, and of corresponding breadth,
and he drove into it thirty iron nails, intending to represent
by them all his Lord's wounds and love-tokens. He placed
this cross upon his bare back between his shoulders on the
flesh, and he bore it continually day and night in honour of
his crucified Lord. . . . The first time that he stretched out
this cross upon his back his tender frame was struck with
terror at it, and he blunted the sharp nails very slightly
upon a stone. But very soon repenting of this unmanly
cowardice, he pointed and sharpened them all again with a
file, and placed the cross once more upon him.

* * * * * *

Therefore, as valiant knights of our imperial Lord, let us
not lose heart; as noble followers of our venerable Leader,
let us be of good cheer, and rejoice to suffer; for if there
were no other profit and good in suffering, than that we
became more like the fair bright mirror Christ, the more
closely that we copied Him in this, our sufferings would be
well laid out. It seems to me in truth, that even if God

meant to give the same reward hereafter to those who suffer and those who do not suffer, we ought still to choose suffering for our lot, were it only to be like Him; for love produces likeness and devotion to the beloved, so far as it can and may.

*   *   *   *   *   *

But the noblest and best kind of suffering is after the pattern of Christ's sufferings—I mean those which the heavenly Father gave to His only-begotten Son, and which He still gives to His dear and chosen friends. This must not be taken as if any one were altogether without fault, except indeed the dear Jesus Christ, who never sinned; but it is to be understood of the example of patience which Christ gave us when He bore Himself in His sufferings like a gentle little lamb among wolves.

✴ Theologia Germanica
[1350]

Luther declared that next to the Bible and St. Augustine, "no book hath ever come into my hands, whence I have learnt, or would wish to learn more of what God, and Christ, and man and all things are." Luther "discovered" it and published an edition in 1516 when he wrote the aforegoing words in the preface. Its appearance a good two hundred years before the Reformation marks the beginning of a shift in thinking that applied the imitation of Christ to any station in life. Though written apparently by a priest, its message appeals to the common people. It lays aside many of the non-essentials of the theology and ecclesiology of the times in exchange for the reality of internal imitation. "Christiform" is the peculiar anglicized form of the word which presents the kernel of its message. "This [man becoming God-like] once took place in the most perfect way in Christ, and every man should become by grace what Christ was by nature." Rather than theorize, we must follow: "But though Christ's life be the most bitter of all, yet it is to be preferred above all . . . for the life of Christ is the best and noblest, the worthiest and loveliest in God's sight that ever was or will be." Thus, participation in the divine nature is the goal, the imitation of Christ the way. The three steps on the medieval mystic ladder are purification, enlightenment, and union. In this work, as is standard for medieval mysticism, imitation of Christ is associated with the first step.

✴

For the Life of Christ Is the Best and Noblest

Behold! this were a good path to the Best, and a noble and blessed preparation for the farthest goal which a man can reach in this temporal world, for the precious life of Christ. For in the life of Christ he walks in the aforesaid ways perfectly and wholly, to the end of his bodily life on earth. Therefore there is no other or better way or preparation to the blissful life of Jesus Christ, than that life itself, and to exercise oneself therein, as much as may be. Of what belongs thereto we have already said somewhat; nay, all that we have here or elsewhere said and written, is but a way or summons to that end. But what the end is, knows no man to declare. But let him who would know it, follow my counsel and take the right way thereto, which is the humble life of Jesus Christ; let him strive after that with unwearied perseverance, and so, without doubt, he shall come to that end which endures forever. For "he that endures to the end shall be saved."

*   *   *   *   *   *

He who knows and recognizes the Christ-life, knows and recognizes Christ also. And in like manner, he who knows not that life, knows not Christ either. He who believes in Christ believes that his life is the best and most precious life that ever was; and if a man believe not this, neither does he believe in Christ. And in so far as the Christ-life is in a man, Christ is in him, and the less of the one, the less of the other. For where there is the Christ-life, there is Christ also, and where his life is not, Christ is not. But where the Christ-life is, the man must say with Saint Paul, "I live, yet not I, but Christ lives in me."

*   *   *   *   *   *

All that has been here said, Christ taught in words and fulfilled in works for three and thirty years. And he teaches it to us very briefly when he says: "Follow me." But he who will follow him, must forsake all things, for in him all things were so wholly forsaken as never in any creature else they were or will be. Moreover, he who will follow him, must take up the cross, and the cross is nothing else than the Christ-life, for that is a bitter cross to all nature. Therefore he says: "He that renounces not all things and takes not up the cross, is not worthy of me, and cannot be my disciple, and follows me not." But false, free nature imagines that it has forsaken all things; yet it will have none of the cross, and says it has had enough of it already, and needs it no longer; and thus is it deceived. For had it ever tasted the cross, it would never forsake it. He that believes in Christ must believe all that is here written.

* * * * * *

Of a truth we ought to know and believe that there is no life so precious and good and well pleasing to God, as the life of Christ, and yet, to nature and selfhood, it is the bitterest life. The careless and free life, on the contrary, is the sweetest and pleasantest life to nature and selfhood and I-hood. But it is not the best; and in many men it may become the worst. But though the Christ-life be the most bitter of all, yet it is to be preferred above all.

* * * * * *

Behold! all that we have said of poverty and humility is so in truth, and we have the proof and witness thereof in the pure life of Christ, and in his words. For he both practiced and fulfilled every work of true humility and all other virtues, as shines forth in his holy life. And he says it also in words: "Learn of me, for I am meek and lowly of heart." . . .

Therefore, where God is the man, and the man is a true follower of Christ, it must needs be the same. But where there is pride, and spiritual wealth, and a light, free mind, Christ is not, nor any true follower of his. Christ said: "My soul is troubled, even unto death." He means his bodily death, in so far as he was born of Mary; until his bodily death, he had not one good day, but only trouble, sorrow, and contrariety. Therefore it is reasonable that it should be even so in his servants. Christ said also: "Blessed are the poor in spirit," (that is, those who are truly humble) "for theirs is the kingdom of Heaven." And thus we find it in truth, where God is man. For in Christ and in his true followers, there must needs be true, thorough humility and poorness of spirit, a contrite and persevering heart, and a soul filled with a secret and hidden sorrowing and lamenting, until the death of the body. And he who imagines otherwise is deceived, and deceives others with him, as we have said. Therefore also all nature and selfhood turn away from this life, and cling to a false, free, and easy life, as we have set forth.

✴ LUDOLPH *of* SAXONY
[d. 1378]

The *Life of Christ* by Ludolph was one of the first in a stream of "biographies" of Jesus which has flowed from the pens of His devotees to this day. This early one made such an impression on medieval thought that it has been called a *summa evangelica*. In it the author condensed all that over sixty writers had said before him on spiritual matters related to the events in Jesus' life. It is, therefore, not a simple biography; it is anything but, since over half of the subject matter is "preaching" by this practical teacher. Ludolph, contrary to the customary approach, which like the Gospels concentrated upon the events of the Passion, devoted two-thirds of his book to the public life of Christ. His manifest purpose in writing this extensive commentary (four volumes in the latest Latin edition) was to show how the perfection of the Christian life consists in self-denial, the carrying of the cross, and the imitation of Christ. Those very topics compose the subhead of a section entitled, "An Exhortation to Follow after Christ and the Example of His Passion." His prayer at the close of the section reads: "Da etiam mihi, ut te sequav, vestigia tua imitando; et tuae vitae me conformando, post te veniam ad supernam patriam pertingend. Amen."

An Exhortation to Follow After Christ

The third level of perfection is the imitation of Christ in the way He preceded us. It must be known that to follow

Christ is nothing more than to imitate His footsteps and to conform to His life. Moreover, we ought to imitate Him in the three ways in which He preceded us, namely: in poverty, in humility and in suffering. For Christ left us, in His coming into the world, an example of most sincere poverty; in His walking through the world, an example of deepest humility; and in His exodus, an example of most bitter suffering. And, because we ought to follow the footsteps of Christ in these three things, He reminds us of the yoke of these three saying: Remember my poverty, in the first place; and my humiliation (i.e., my deepest condescension), in the second place; and my wormwood and gall (i.e., my most bitter passion), in the third place. And remember that all who are devoted to evangelical perfection ought to imitate Christ and to conform to His likeness in terms of these conditions, which are given to us by God: that is, to renounce external things, the body itself, and even the ego. It is necessary that all be left for the sake of God if we wish to be perfect imitators of Christ.

For the perfect imitator of Christ ought, first, to relinquish the world and all temporal interests, and also he ought to put away preoccupation with earthly matters and anxiety about inward concerns. One does this through undertaking voluntary poverty which Christ served most highly, as He was very poor throughout His entire life. In the second place, the perfect imitator ought to subjugate the body in three ways: first, by flagellating the body, which is accomplished by watching, fasting and prayer, in order that the flesh be not wanton and rise up presumptuously and stubbornly against the spirit; second, by renouncing worldly possessions because anyone who is a slave to his own comforts, i.e. his body, will afterward perceive it contaminated; therefore it should always be held in restraint in order that it may be the more subject to the spirit; third, by assuming voluntary sufferings just as the Apostles and martyrs who suffered freely for Christ. Thus Christ did these things and gave Himself as an example. In the third place, the perfect imitator of Christ ought to abandon his own self, by the rejection of his very will, in order that he may conform himself to the divine will, wishing nothing except that which pleases God. For thus did Christ, who said, "I came not to do my will, but the will of him who sent me." For in the divine will, you have rules and regulations for all your actions, that you may desire nothing except that which in you and in all other creatures glorifies God.

Spiritual death, according to the example of Christ, is accomplished in five steps. For it must be announced that no one is able to live by the life of Christ who is not ready to die like Christ. Therefore, even as Christ sought to die in a certain manner, to accomplish which, He out of His excessive love submitted to the human form and emptied Himself. . . . So anyone striving toward this perfection ought through true humility and full disdain for his own death to consider himself nothing in order that he may be able to live for God alone. Moreover, he ought to regard highly this way which is given him by God, namely, conformity to the life of Christ, and to watch with the greatest diligence in order that he may be able to say with the Apostle: "I live; yet not I, but Christ liveth in me" . . . All the foregoing steps of self contempt are most favorably shone forth in Christ. Therefore, let us follow straightway and let us not imitate the devil, being ambitious and prideful; nor the world, being greedy and avaricious; nor the fleshly appetites, being voluptuous and lascivious; but imitate the Lord Jesus Christ. For whosoever does not follow God indeed, does not proceed to deny himself for Him, nor to bear the cross. Do you wish to follow Christ? Then be obedient to God; next, be diligent; and bear and do all things for the sake of

God, by abstaining from evil and pursuing virtue. For Christ trod in this path; therefore walk in this way, if you wish to follow Him in the present life and to rejoice with Him in the next. But, behold, few today wish to follow Christ; nonetheless many wish to come to Him!

✳ GERARD GROOTE
[1340–1384]

"Oh! noble man, who was girt with a rough shirt of hair, and, like Christ, robed in the cloak of holy poverty . . . He even walked upon the path of humility under the leadership of Christ, and conformed his life by rule to the pattern of the Saints of old." So Thomas à Kempis, writing in *The Founders of the New Devotion*, described its earliest leader. Groote, influenced directly by Ruysbroeck and other mystics, went beyond them to the primitive Church and the Gospel. The fundamental rule of the Brethren of the Common Life, as they were called, was: "Let the root of thy study and the mirror of thy life be in the first place the Gospel of Christ, because there is the life of Christ." While teaching was one of their duties (they instructed Erasmus, for instance), they thought life is learned more in imitating the lowly Jesus than in reading all the books. They taught men to become true disciples of Christ instead of Masters of Arts, to labor with one's hands like Paul, to have community of goods like the Christians in Acts, and to confess sins mutually. They put aside the title "master" and lived in simple fashion among the poor working class. Of Groote it is reported that he gave up prebends, ceded his house to godly women, returned good for evil, and devoted years to hard labor alongside the poor. The spirit of the group is best stated by à Kempis: "The imitation of Jesus is the life of holy humility, self-denial, and affectionate labour for others. . . . Receive Christ, let Him be formed within thee, follow and imitate His example, and with Him thou hast all."

Groote attacked especially false shepherds. "Bartholomew," he reported of one of them, "enters inns and gets many friends there, for he finds fault with no one. Nothing is so dangerous as to preach about God and perfection, and not to point out the way which leads to perfection. Penitence is hardly necessary in his opinion; tell him that if he is to preach any longer, he must show the people the way to heaven through Christ by following in His footsteps, not by ignoring the imperfections of men, and the existence of sin." His was a practical and Bible-centered theology, but though carefully orthodox, he was silenced by the authorities for exposing the evils of churchmen in the light of the purity of the life of Christ.

On Patience: Via Dolores

Hence this is what I teach continuously and everywhere: that the Passion of our Lord Jesus Christ must always be remembered, because no evil can happen to anyone who faces adversity in this frame of mind. Not only must it be remembered so that through meditation it may be present in our intellect, but even more let us through imitation of His sufferings, reproaches, and hardships possess it in our disposition; in order that as Christians we may rise through conformity to Christ in works and deeds. For on account of this desire and disposition, when the mind finds the occasion it will wish to be crucified, to suffer and to be rebuked with Christ. And finally and principally, meditation upon the Passion of Christ must produce imitation; for the memory alone of the Passion is of little value if it is not accompanied by a strong desire to imitate Christ. . . .

In such fashion, a person denies himself and bears his own cross, and follows Christ. For the cross of Christ is nothing more than voluntary assumption of the hardships, sufferings, and reproaches by which the world is crucified by man (that is to say, those things which are worldly are despised by the Christian) and he himself by the world (that is, he is despised by the world and afflicted by worldly men). This cross, conforming to the Cross of the Lord Jesus Christ, branches from it through us like a river from its fountain, like a spoke from its axle. But behold! many of us assume willingly crosses which we make for ourselves whether in wearing cowls, whether in private prayer, or whether in individual fasting; but those crosses God makes for us are the real ones and must in truth be borne and honored by us. The fact is, though, we do not bear the real crosses voluntarily; indeed, we cast them abhoringly from us.

Above all it is indeed necessary for us to bear God-given crosses without recalcitrance and murmurings, and on the contrary to despise all those things which we feign to be crosses and, if you please, have their own reward. For what is more manful than to break one's own will, and what is more divine and more sobering than to conform to the will of God? . . . For the cross of Christ must be forged in us continuously by thinking on the Passion. And insults, derisions, injuries and sufferings must be continuously striven after. . . . This must be done mainly from desire for honor and conformity to Jesus Christ without respect for rewards and prizes. Therefore, that you may be the richer in rewards, but not mercenary about it, be conformed to Christ and offer yourself humbly to Him and through Him to the Father; be received, continue and be perfected, not in your own strength but in the manner and merits of Christ.

GERARD ZERBOLT
[1367-1398]

THOMAS à KEMPIS
[1380-1471]

"The Imitation of Christ is a voice rising out of the darkness to remind us that the Church of Christ never ceased to exist, but that God had His witnesses and Christ His lovers even in the era of deepest decay," declared James Stalker. Scholars are of the opinion that Thomas à Kempis is not the single author of the classic, but is rather the editor of Groote's spiritual diary. Groote, as we have seen, spearheaded that movement among the Christians of the Lowlands which exposed the form of imitation by the "religious" and which sought to apply the Way of Christ to the whole of life. Zerbolt and à Kempis were followers in that group which combined the mystical and the practical in devotion. It is the opinion of Professor Albert Hyma that the original First Book of the four-book Imitation appears in its purest and most robust form in the manuscript ascribed to Gerard Zerbolt. In other words, it seems that the stringent appeal of via dolores is toned down even in the famous and multiplied Thomas edition! For that reason, the excerpts from Book I have been taken from the Hyma translation of Zerbolt's rendition.

Irrespective of the dispute concerning authorship and the quality of editing, the classic sets forth the universal challenge of complete discipleship. The true prayer of the Christian is: "Lord Jesus, forasmuch as thy life was poor and contemptible unto the world, grant me grace to imitate thee in suffering worldly contempt. For the servant is not greater than his

89

Lord, nor the disciple above his Master. Let thy servant be exercised in thy life, for therein my salvation and true holiness consist."

The theology and ethic of the volume are contained in the following paragraph: "For Thy life is our way, and by holy patience we walk toward Thee who art our Crown. If Thou hadst not gone before us and taught us, who would have gone the way which Thou hast traced out? Alas! how many would stay behind and remain far off, if they beheld not Thy glorious example! Behold, we are still cold, although we have heard of so many of Thy miracles and doctrines; what would become of us, if we had not so great a light given us to follow Thee?"

Bk. I, Ch. I. Of the Imitation of Our Lord Jesus Christ.

1. "He that followeth Me, walketh not in darkness," says the Lord. (John 8:12).

2. These are the words of Christ, by which we are admonished how we ought to imitate His life and manners, if we will be truly enlightened, and be delivered from all blindness of heart.

3. Let therefore our chief endeavor be to imitate Jesus in our life. . . .

20. Endeavor therefore to withdraw your heart from all love of visible things, for many offer promises, but few make good. . . . Turn your attention to invisible things, and start a better life, in order that you may thus imitate Christ, for every deed of His is an instruction for us. And speak with Job: "My foot hath held fast to his steps." (Job 23:11). . . .

Ch. XVIII. On the Examples of the Fathers.

4. So these and others, in slander and abuse patiently bore punishments and outrages—prophets, apostles, martyrs, confessors, virgins, widows and many men who followed the footsteps of Christ and for His love fervently shed their red blood. . . .

Ch. XXV. On Fervent Correction.

7. Be mindful of a firm proposal and consider the life of Christ.

8. And be ashamed for not yet have you fashioned yourself more greatly after Him—you who have been so long His imitator.

9. Consider His most bitter death and passion, and each day recall the whole span of His life, how through thirty-three years He spent His time in every misery and toil, in weariness and cold, in travel, in watches, fasts, abstinence and prayer, how He walked with bare head and feet.

10. When you were weary, He was your consolation, for He did all these things for your sake.

11. If you say you love Him you must prove by the evidence of your works that your friend is cheap who shows you no sign of charity.

12. And you may know that the devoted memory of Christ's passion is of more value than the traveling upon all the earth, the daily reading of the whole psalter, the scourging of one's whole body.

13. Therefore let us bear in our hearts what He endured for us in His body, that we who are participants in His passion and suffering might become also companions in His glory and merits. . . .

16. Oh slothful one, may you weary of continuing in

sin. Rise up you who sleep and Jesus Christ will enlighten you.

17. Pattern your life to that of such devoted ones. If you desire their end, take up also their life. . . .

22. Willingly follow Him who will crown you frequently in the future, for great is His glory: follow the Lord.

*   *   *   *   *   *

Bk. II, Ch. XI. That there are few who love the Cross of Christ.

1. Jesus hath many lovers of His heavenly kingdom; but few bearers of His Cross.

He hath many desirous of comfort, but few of tribulation.

He findeth many companions of His table, but few of His abstinence.

All desire to rejoice with Him, few will suffer any thing for Him.

Many follow Jesus unto the breaking of bread, but few to the drinking of the cup of His passion.

Many reverence his miracles, few follow the ignominy of His Cross.

Many love Jesus, as long as adversities happen not: Many praise and bless Him, as long as they receive any comfort from Him.

But if Jesus hide Himself, and leave them but a while, they fall either into complaint or into dejection.

2. But they that love Jesus for Jesus, and not for some comfort of their own, bless Him in all tribulation and anguish of heart, as well as in the greatest comfort.

Ch. XII. Of the Royal Way of the Holy Cross.

1. This speech seemeth hard to many, "Renounce thyself, take up thy Cross, and follow Jesus." But it will be much

harder to hear that last word, "Depart from me, ye cursed, into everlasting fire." . . .

They that now willingly follow the doctrine of the Cross, shall not then fear to hear the sentence of everlasting damnation. This sign of the Cross shall be in heaven, when our Lord shall come to judgment. . . .

2. Why therefore fearest thou to take up the Cross, which leadeth to a kingdom?

> In the Cross is salvation; in the Cross is life,
> in the Cross is protection against our enemies,
> in the Cross is heavenly sweetness,
> in the Cross is strength of mind,
> in the Cross is joy of spirit,
> in the Cross is the height of virtue,
> in the Cross is the perfection of holiness.

There is no salvation of the soul, nor hope of everlasting life, but in the Cross.

Take up therefore thy Cross and follow Jesus, and thou shalt go into life everlasting. He is gone before bearing His Cross, and is dead for thee on the Cross; that thou mayest also bear thy Cross, and desire to die on the Cross with Him.

3. Go where thou wilt, seek wheresoever thou wilt, thou shalt not find a higher way above, nor a safer way below, than the way of the Holy Cross.

4. No man hath so cordial a feeling of the passion of Christ, as he who hath suffer'd the like himself.

Both above and below, without and within, which way soever thou dost turn thee, everywhere thou shalt find the Cross; and everywhere of necessity thou must have patience, if thou wilt have inward peace, and enjoy an everlasting crown.

5. If thou bear the Cross willingly, it will bear thee.

6. Verily, Jesus Christ our Lord was never one hour with-

out suffering, so long as He lived. Christ (saith He) ought to suffer, and rise again from the dead, and so enter into His glory. And dost thou seek any other way than this royal way, which is the way of the Holy Cross?

7. The whole life of Christ was a Cross and a Martyrdom; and dost thou seek rest and joy? . . .

12. It remaineth therefore, that thou suffer, if thou wilt love Jesus, and perpetually serve Him. . . .

14. Nothing is more grateful unto God, nothing more wholesome to thee in the world, than to suffer willingly for Christ. And if it were in thy choice, thou shouldst rather wish to suffer adversities for Christ, than to enjoy many comforts; because hereby thou shouldst be more like Christ, and more conformable to all the saints.

15. If anything had been better and more profitable to the salvation of man than suffering, Christ surely would have shewed it by word and example. But He plainly exhorteth all that follow Him, to the bearing of the Cross, and saith, If any will come after me, let him renounce himself, and take up his Cross, and follow me.

DESIDERIUS ERASMUS
[1466?–1536]

That the imitation theme should appear in Renaissance man may seem strange, but at least the fact attests to its manifold appeal. As it is expounded by Erasmus, it harbingers the modern rational attempt to reduce Christianity to "its minimum," oversimplified as the religion of Jesus and the Sermon on the Mount ethic. Erasmus' recommendation at the outset of his *Manual of the Christian Knight* might well be considered his own task: "Therefore in mine opinion the best were that some both well learned men and good of living should have this office assigned and put unto them, to make a collection and to gather the sum of Christ's philosophy out of the pure fountain of the gospel and the epistles and most approved interpreters, and so plainly that yet it might be clerkly and erudite, and so briefly that it might also be plain." Christ, uncovered from dogma and the Pope, should be made the center of circles: "Therefore the mark must be set before every man which they ought to shoot at: and there is but one mark, which is Christ and his most pure learning . . ." Certainly we would expect thoughts like these from the mind of a refined literary personage imbued in the classics revived by the Renaissance. Nonetheless, he held to "the chief mark, to follow Christ's living." The Fourth Rule of the book cited is the principal line: "That thou have Christ always in thy sight as the only mark of all thy living and conversation, unto whom only thou shouldst direct all thine enforcements, all thy pastimes and purposes, all thy rest and quietness, and also thy business." Though no radical reformer, it seems that he remembered well the lesson of his teachers, the Brethren of the Common Life.

A literary gem carved by Erasmus on the imitation of Christ standard is addressed to children and entitled "A Sermon on the Child Jesus." Jesus, the Child among children, the Pattern of their life, the Captain of the youthful band, is ever the central figure. The gist of the sermon is: "Wherefore, truly and with heart, not with only words, we love Jesus, let us endeavor for our power to express Jesus; or rather to be transformed into him. And if we cannot follow the man, let us children follow the child."

A Sermon on the Child Jesus

Christianity is none other thing in the world but a certain new birth, which in the Bible is called a regeneration; and that is none other thing save a being a child again. . . . Wherefore there is also a certain new kind of childhood, which is allowed of Christ; a childhood without childishness; and, generally to speak, a certain aged childhood, which standeth not in the number of years, but in innocence and simplicity of wit. . . . Wherefore to these gifts of nature if imitation of that high and absolute child be added, then finally shall children seem loving and kind towards him, and also worthy and fit for him: for the child that so deserveth who can not but love? Undoubtedly, such is the virtue and violent operation of true love, that thou wilt covet to be so like as may be possible unto the thing which thou lovest. Which thing if human love worketh in us, what zeal of following shall divine love kindle?

*　　*　　*　　*　　*　　*

Verily I see that there be three things principally, which be wont to kindle and enflame the hearts either of scholars or of soldiers, to do valiantly and manly. The first is, to be brought in to an admiration of their guide or captain; the second, to love him; the third, the reward. Wherefore, to that intent we might with more fervent and cheerful courage obey our master and captain Jesus, go we to. Let us consider severally all these three things with a devout curiosity in him. First of all, how wonderful he is on every side, and to be astonished at. After that, how greatly he is to be loved, and for that cause also to be followed. And last of all, what high profit, fruit, and advantage shall arise unto us by this love.

* * * * * *

But here again thou, oh! good Jesu, with what unspeakable providence, with what unheard an example, with what incomparable charity, hast thou restored that work that thou didst create. . . . Thou tookest upon thee our humanity, to call us to the fellowship of thy divinity. . . . Furthermore, throughout all the whole process of thy most holy life, with how lively examples dost thou enflame our hearts? With how wholesome precepts dost thou nurture and form us? With how wonderful miracles dost thou awaken us? With how fair monitions dost thou draw us? With how sure promises dost thou invite? So that there is none more commodious way to thee than by thy own self; which only art *the way, the truth, and life.*

* * * * * *

Wherefore, bearing ourselves bold of this grace, let us with a great heart and stomach enterprise the study to follow the child Jesus; and let us never move our eyes from him; being . . . our mark. We have a perfect and an absolute exemplar: there is nothing else to be sought. All his life continually crieth what we ought to do. For what teacheth us that most pure child, that he was born of a most pure virgin, but to eschew all filth and defoulments of this world, and to meditate a certain angelical life even now in earth; that is, to meditate that here, which there we shall be continually? . . . What taught he us, in that he was borne from home in another country, delivered of his mother in a vile cottage, cast down in a crib, wrapped about with vile clothes, but that we should always remember that we be here strangers for a few days; and that, all riches trodden under feet, and the false honors of the whole world despised. . . ?

Now consider ye with ourselves, oh! children, with how holy studies and occupations that same child, so born, so offered up to God, did pass over his childhood. Not with idleness, not with eating and drinking, not with sleep, not with vain sports and plays, not with foolish fables, not with strayings abroad . . . but either with ministering and serving his parents, or with holy prayers, or hearing the preachers and teachers, or with devout meditations, or with holy and earnest communications with other children. . . . For no age is unripe to learn holiness; nay rather, none other age is more timely and meet to learn Christ, than that which knoweth not yet the world.

MARTIN LUTHER
[1483–1546]

Transcending both the lip service of the perfunctory ecclesiastics and the works-salvation of the monastics, Luther,
with an earthy vividness and a profound religious feeling for
the human life of Jesus Christ, held imitation at the center
of his preaching. "To 'put on Christ' may be understood in
two ways, according to the Law and according to the Gospel.
According to the Law as in Romans 13:14, which means to
follow the example of Christ. To put on Christ according to
the Gospel means to clothe oneself with the righteousness,
wisdom, power, life and spirit of Christ. . . . When we have
put on the robe of righteousness of Christ we must not forget
to put on also the mantle of the imitation of Christ." Thus,
in either case, imitation cannot be evaded. But Luther as
much as any person saw Christ in His exemplar office as something more than Teacher or good moral Portrait: "Christ
alone as Example is to me a measure; by it I measure myself,
i. e., as lawgiver and judge. Example alone has not freed; it
teaches, challenges, embarrasses, harasses: hardly a hundredth
or a thousandth part of this Example have I fulfilled."

Luther recaptured the time-honored formula, *sacramentum
et exemplum*, and made it the key to his interpretation: "The
Scriptures present Christ in a twofold aspect. First, as a gift.
. . . Secondly, as an example. As an exemplar He is to be
placed before me only at certain times. In times of joy and
gladness that I may have Him as a mirror to reflect upon
my shortcomings. But in the day of trouble I will have Christ
only as a gift." In his emphasis upon the *exemplum* side,
which the high Christology since Luther has often over-
looked, he stressed both the judgment involved in the attempt

to imitate and the necessity of entering into Christ's sufferings. This latter note, the appropriation unto ourselves of the Saviour, especially His sufferings, he borrowed from the mystics in whom he had been thoroughly schooled; and he often quoted their phrase: "What happened in Christ, must happen also in us."

A fresh approach to imitation comes in Luther's classic, *Christian Liberty*. Here imitation is introduced as *being* Christ to our fellow creatures: "I will therefore give myself as a Christ to my neighbor, just as Christ offered Himself to me. . . . Each should become as it were a Christ to the other, that we may be Christs to one another and Christ may be the same in all; that is that we may be truly Christians."

One final word of caution Luther would offer, which arises from his rediscovery of the authority of the Bible: "For whatever He desired that we should do or suffer, He not merely did and suffered Himself, but also declared by His word that we should imitate. Therefore, we hold no example so binding, not even the example of Christ, unless it agrees with the word of God, which expounds to us what we should follow and what we should not follow."

Luther excelled in his pastoral preaching; it is significant that he held the *imitatio* ideal before the whole congregation, not just for the clergy as had been standard for generations.

AN EXHORTATION TO PATIENCE BY CHRIST'S EXAMPLE
I Peter 2:21

Here mark you, is the example set before the entire Christian Church, the pattern she is to follow to the extent of at least walking in Christ's steps, at the same time, however, remembering that her most intense sufferings are naught in comparison to a single drop of his shed blood . . . Where these two principals of the Christian doctrine are not maintained in their proper relation, injury must result to the truth in two respects: they who are occupied solely with their own works corrupt the true doctrine of faith; they who neglect to follow the example of Christ retard the efficacy and fruit of that faith. . . .

Mark the example of Christ, however, and there learn to censure yourself. Wicked, unprofitable and condemned servant must he be who does not follow his Lord's example of endurance but presumes to think himself better and nobler than Christ; who with inimical spirit murmurs, complaining of great injustice, when he really deserves afflictions, and when he suffers infinitely less than did his dear, righteous, innocent Lord. Beloved, if Christ so suffered in return for the great blessing he conferred, be not too indolent to imitate him in some degree by suffering without anger and reproaches.

*   *   *   *   *   *

For when one flees and becomes a monk, it sounds as though he were saying, "Pfui! How the people stink! How damnable is their state! I will be saved, and let them go to the devil!" If Christ had fled thus and become such a holy monk, who would have died for us or rendered satisfaction for us poor sinners? Would it have been the monks, with their strict lives of flight?

True, St. John the Baptist was in the wilderness, though not entirely away from people; but afterwards, when he had reached man's estate, he came back among people and preached. Christ—like Moses on Mount Sinai—was forty days quite apart from men in the wilderness and neither ate nor drank; but He, too, came back among the people. Well, then, let us hold them for hermits and monks if we like; and yet neither of them condemns paid soldiers as a class, but John says to them, "Be satisfied with your wages and do no one violence or wrong." Christ went to the centurion at Capernaum, in order to help his servant, who served, beyond a doubt, for pay, and Christ does not call his class lost, but praises his faith above all Israel; and St. Peter allowed Cornelius, at Caesarea, to remain centurion after his baptism, together with his servants, who were there in the pay of the Romans. How much less, then, ought St. Anthony and his monks to have cast a stench upon this ordinance of God, with his new and peculiar holiness; since he was a simple layman, wholly unlearned, and was not a preacher and held no office in the Church. To be sure, I believe that he was great before God, as were many others of his pupils; but the thing he undertook is full of offense and dangerous, though he was preserved in it, as the elect are preserved amid sins and other offenses. Nevertheless, it is not the example of his life that is to be praised, but the example and teaching of Christ and John.

IGNATIUS LOYOLA

[1491–1556]

In Ignatius, medieval chivalry and militarism are directed into religious channels. The famous *Exercises*, one commentator has said, "are just *The Imitation* martialled in battle array." It is unquestioned that during the period of his spiritual crisis he was influenced by the *imitatio* stream of thought. For while he was convalescing after the battle of Pampeluna, Ludolph's book fell into his hands, and later at Manresa, he came under the influence of *The Imitation*. In writing his book of discipline he recommended the latter strongly.

Well known is his resolve to become a knight for Christ. Soon thereafter, he longed to visit the Holy Land where the Master had walked. In an impulsive moment, he put in jeopardy the entire Christian community, which was under Turkish occupation, by trespassing at night into the Mount of Olives, where he put his feet in the venerated footprints of the Saviour! His one desire was to imitate Christ. On the long voyage home, he came to the realization that in order to do that better he must learn the life of Christ, and hence the Scriptures. Accordingly, he returned to school and the study of Latin. But he chose à Kempis instead of Erasmus and became a man of action in the world rather than a monk. Thus the Order of the Jesuits (1540) was born, and *The Spiritual Exercises* (1541), devised to train the Christian Knight in twenty-eight days for arduous battles. Father Rickaby holds that "the lesson of the Exercises is not prayer, nor alms-deeds, nor austerities, nor zeal for souls; it is love of humiliations, detachment from creatures, and burning

103

personal love of Jesus Christ." In them he is said to have
fathered the retreat idea.

Perfect obedience to the will and mission of God is his
aim; the life of Christ is to be imitated because He perfectly
obeyed. "From beginning to end, from Incarnation to Calvary,
the life of Jesus is dominated by the law of obedience. . . .
For it is the example of Christ that has inspired the great
heroes of the religious life to achieve the renowned exploits
which have made their obedience so famous." In his famous
Letter on Obedience (Rome, 1553) he formalized the chief
mark of imitation by his Order: "We may allow ourselves to
be surpassed by other religious orders in fasts, watchings, and
other austerities, which each one following its Institute holily
embraces; but in the purity and perfection of obedience,
joined to the true resignation of our wills and the abnegation
of our judgment, I am very desirous, dear brethren, that they
who serve God in this Society should be conspicuous . . ."

The first Point is, to put before me a human king chosen
by God our Lord, whom all Christian princes and men
reverence and obey.

The second, to look how this king speaks to all his people,
saying: "It is my Will to conquer all the land of unbelievers.
Therefore, whoever would like to come with me is to be content to eat as I, and also to drink and dress, etc., as I: likewise
he is to labor like me in the day and watch in the night, etc.,
that so afterwards he may have part with me in the victory,
as he has had it in the labors."

The third, to consider what the good subjects ought to
answer to a king so liberal and so kind, and hence, if any
one did not accept the appeal of such a king, how deserving

he would be of being censured by all the world, and held for
a mean-spirited knight.

*   *   *   *   *   *

The second part of this Exercise consists in applying the
above parable of the temporal king to Christ our Lord, con-
formably to the three points mentioned. . . .

"Eternal Lord of all things, I make my oblation with Thy
favor and help, in presence of Thy infinite Goodness and in
presence of Thy glorious Mother and of all the Saints of the
heavenly Court; that I want and desire, and it is my deliberate
determination, if only it be Thy greater service and praise, to
imitate Thee in bearing all injuries and all abuse and all
poverty of spirit, and actual poverty, too, if Thy most Holy
Majesty wants to choose and receive me to such life and
state."

*   *   *   *   *   *

The first Prelude is the narrative. It will be here how Christ
calls and wants all under His standard; and Lucifer, on the
contrary, under his.

The second, a composition, seeing the place. It will be here
to see a great field of all that region of Jerusalem, where the
supreme Commander-in-chief of the good is Christ our
Lord . . .

The third, to ask for what I want . . . for knowledge of the
true life which the supreme and true Captain shows and
grace to imitate Him. . . .

So, on the contrary, one has to imagine as to the supreme
and true Captain, Who is Christ our Lord.

The first Point is to consider how Christ our Lord puts
Himself in a great field of that region of Jerusalem, in lowly
place, beautiful and attractive.

The second, to consider how the Lord of all the world

chooses so many persons—Apostles, Disciples, etc.,—and sends them through all the world spreading His sacred doctrine through all states and conditions of persons.

The third, to consider the discourse which Christ our Lord makes to all His servants and friends whom He sends on this expedition, recommending them to want to help all, by bringing them first to the highest spiritual poverty, and—if His Divine Majesty would be served and would want to choose them—no less to actual poverty; the second is to be of contumely and contempt; because from these two things humility follows. So that there are to be three steps; the first, poverty against riches; the second, contumely or contempt against worldly honor; the third, humility against pride. And from these three steps let them induce to all the other virtues.

One Colloquy to Our Lady, that she may get me grace from Her Son and Lord that I may be received under His standard; and first in the highest spiritual poverty, and—if His Divine Majesty would be served and would want to choose and receive me—not less in actual poverty; second, in suffering contumely and injuries, to imitate Him more in them . . .

*   *   *   *   *   *

The third [Humility] is most perfect Humility; namely, when—including the first and second, and the praise and glory of the Divine Majesty being equal—in order to imitate and be more actually like Christ our Lord, I want and choose poverty with Christ poor rather than riches, opprobrium with Christ replete with it rather than honors; and to desire to be rated as worthless and a fool for Christ, Who first was held as such, rather than wise or prudent in this world.

✳ JOHN CALVIN
[1509–1564]

Of the standard theologians, perhaps the reader is most surprised that Calvin appears in the procession of those who imitated Christ. To be sure, he wrote with a legalistically trained mind, but certain passages of his *Institutes of the Christian Religion* attain lyrical heights, markedly those having to do with the person of Christ and the life of a Christian. The section called "The Summary of the Christian Life" is unexcelled in its description of Christlike self-denial for the good of one's neighbor. From it comes the classic sentence: "For we shall never arrive at true meekness (like Christ's) by any other way, than by having our hearts imbued with self-abasement and a respect for others." Moreover, a poem composed by him in 1560 comes up to its title, "Salutation to Jesus Christ," as the following lines reveal:

> I greet thee, my Redeemer sure,
>   I trust in none but thee,
> Thou who hast borne such toil and shame
>   And suffering for me:
> Our hearts from cares and cravings vain
>   And foolish fears set free.

>   *   *   *   *   *   *

> Thou art the life by which we live;
>   Our stay and strength's in thee;
> Uphold us so in face of death,
>   What time soe'er it be,
> That we may meet it with strong heart,
>   And may die peacefully.

The true and perfect gentleness
  We find in thee alone;
Make us to know thy loveliness,
  Teach us to love thee known;
Grant us sweet fellowship with thee,
  And all who are thine own.

His own life was such an exemplary one that Theodore
Beza, a close friend for sixteen years, could say that "in him
was proposed for the imitation of us all a most beautiful
example of a truly Christian life and death." Calvin had
written: "Only those can be called disciples of Christ who
truly imitate Him and are prepared to follow in His footsteps.
He has given us a summary rule of discipleship so that we
may know in what the imitation of Him essentially consists:
namely, self-denial and the willing bearing of His Cross."

SUMMARY OF THE CHRISTIAN LIFE

A. *Self-Denial.*

And as a further incitement to us, [the Incarnation] shows,
that as God the Father has reconciled us to himself in Christ,
so he has exhibited to us in him a pattern, to which it is his
will that we should be conformed.

If we are not our own, but the Lord's, it is manifest both
what error we must avoid, and to what end all the actions of
our lives are to be directed. We are not our own; therefore
neither our reason nor our will should predominate in our
deliberations and actions. We are not our own; therefore

let us not propose it as our end, to seek what may be expedient for us according to the flesh. We are not our own; therefore let us, as far as possible, forget ourselves and all things that are ours. On the contrary, we are God's; to him, therefore, let us live and die. We are God's; therefore let his wisdom and will preside in all our actions. We are God's; towards him, therefore, as our only legitimate end, let every part of our lives be directed. . . .

B. Respect for Others.

This is that denial of ourselves, which Christ, from the commencement of their course, so diligently enjoins on his disciples; which, when it has once obtained the government of the heart, leaves room neither for pride, haughtiness, or ostentation, nor for avarice, libidinousness, luxury, effeminacy, or any other evils which are the offspring of self-love. On the contrary, wherever it does not reign, there either the grossest vices are indulged without the least shame; or, if there exist any appearance of virtue, it is vitiated by a depraved passion for glory. Show me, if you can, a single individual, who, unless he has renounced himself according to the command of the Lord, is voluntarily disposed to practise virtue among men. For all who have not been influenced by this disposition, have followed virtue merely from the love of praise. . . .

This is the only way of attaining that which is not only difficult, but utterly repugnant to the nature of man—to love them who hate us, to requite injuries with kindnesses, and to return blessings for curses. We should remember, that we must not reflect on the wickedness of men, but contemplate the Divine image in them; which, concealing and obliterating their faults, by its beauty and dignity allures us to embrace them in the arms of our love.

C. Bearing the Cross.

But it becomes a pious mind to rise still higher, even to that to which Christ calls his disciples; that every one should "take up his cross." For all whom the Lord has chosen and honoured with admission into the society of his saints, ought to prepare themselves for a life, hard, laborious, unquiet, and replete with numerous and various calamities. It is the will of their heavenly Father to exercise them in this manner, that he may have a certain proof of those that belong to him. Having begun with Christ his first begotten Son, he pursues this method towards all his children. For though Christ was above all others the beloved Son, in whom the Father was always well pleased, yet we see how little indulgence and tenderness he experienced; so that it may be truly said, not only that he was perpetually burdened with a cross during his residence on earth, but that his whole life was nothing but a kind of perpetual cross. The apostle assigns the reason, that it was necessary for him to "learn obedience by the things which he suffered." Why, then, should we exempt ourselves from that condition, to which it behoved Christ our head to be subject; especially since his submission was on our account, that he might exhibit to us an example of patience in his own person? Wherefore the apostle teaches, that it is the destination of all the children of God "to be conformed to him." It is also a source of signal consolation to us, in unpleasant and severe circumstances, which are esteemed adversities and calamities, that we partake of the sufferings of Christ; that as he from a labyrinth of all evils entered into the glory of heaven, so we are conducted forward through various tribulations to the same glory; for Paul teaches us, that when we "know the fellowship of his sufferings," we also apprehend "the power of his resurrection;" that while we are conformed to his death, we are thus prepared to partake of his glorious resurrection. How much is this adapted to alleviate all the bitterness of the cross, that the more we are afflicted by adversities, our fellowship with Christ is so much the more certainly confirmed! By this communion the sufferings themselves not only become blessings to us, but afford considerable assistance towards promoting our salvation.

✱ TERESA of AVILA
[1515–1582]

Here is no stained-glass saint. " 'Rest, indeed!' I would say. 'I need no rest; what I need is crosses.' " This is reported in her own account, *Life*, describing how she warred against easy religion and introduced the austere and menial life into the sophisticated convents of her Spain. She was virile: following her admonition, "Be strong men," she established over seventeen "foundations" (or convents), once she overcame the opposition to her innovations. She was practical: "From foolish devotions may God deliver us" was her way of saying that contemplation which becomes an end in itself, apart from the desire to practice the Way of Christ, is vain. She was manly: she wrote militant poetry.

> A Captain brave to do and dare,
> Our God was pleased on earth to die,
> So let us follow manfully . . .

Teresa was associated with convent life throughout her years, having been educated there, having taken the vows at twenty-one, and having become the Mother Superior of Carmel and founder of many others. However, she did not rest easy in her vow, and after "twenty years on the stormy sea" of tension she made a vow for complete perfection. This "final conversion" marked the turning point of her life. She reported, "I saw Christ at my side." Her contact with the Jesuits along with this experience enabled her to have intermittently thereafter "visible meditations" upon the Humanity of Christ accompanied by visions. But she harnessed these visions to a life of rigorous action. Besides organizing

112

new types of convents, she wrote incessantly. Her *Life* ranks
with the great Christian journals; and her other major works,
Interior Castle, Way of Perfection, and *Foundations,* are
classics in their own right. Her enthusiasm for Jesus produced
a small commentary on the Canticles called *Conceptions of
Love of God,* fashioned on the medieval pattern. "But one
of her confessors, thinking it a new and dangerous thing that a
woman should write on the Song of Songs, ordered this book
to be burned." Teresa was not easily subdued; her Christianity
was rooted in imitation. "Others . . . will be led by Him along
another way, but I should always choose the way of suffering,
if only to imitate our Lord Jesus Christ."

We need to cultivate, and think upon, and seek the companionship of those who, though living on earth like ourselves, have accomplished such great deeds for God; the last
thing we should do is to withdraw of set purpose from our
greatest help and blessing, which is the most sacred Humanity
of Our Lord Jesus Christ. . . . for, if they lose their Guide,
the good Jesus, they will be unable to find their way; they
will do well if they are able to remain securely in other
Mansions. For the Lord Himself says that He is the Way . . .
For life is long and there are many trials in it and we have
need to look at Christ our Pattern, and also at His Apostles
and Saints, and to reflect how they bore these trials, so that
we, too, may bear them perfectly. The good Jesus is too
good company for us to forsake Him . . .

* * * * * *

Therefore, Sir, even if you reach the summit of contemplation Your Reverence must seek no other way: that way alone

is safe. It is through this Lord of ours that all blessings come. He will show us the way; we must look at His life—that is our best pattern. What more do we need than to have at our side so good a Friend, Who will not leave us in trials and tribulations, as earthly friends do? Blessed is he who loves Him in truth and has Him always at his side.

* * * * * *

What are we nuns doing in our convent? What motive had we for leaving the world? For what purpose have we come here? In what can we better employ ourselves than in making a dwelling-place for our Spouse within the soul, and doing so in time to be able to ask Him for the kiss of His mouth? . . . Oh, my daughters, what a high calling is ours, since none save our own selves can forbid us to address these words to our Spouse, Whom we took as such when we were professed!

* * * * * *

Let us not, then, lament our fears, or be discouraged at the weakness of our human nature and at our lack of strength; let us try rather to fortify ourselves with humility and understand clearly how little we can do by our own efforts. We must realize that if God does not give us this favour we are nothing, so we must have no confidence whatever in our own strength, but trust in His mercy—and until we do this all is weakness. It was not without good reason that Our Lord showed us this. He, of course, had no weakness, for He was fortitude itself; He did it for our comfort and in order that we might learn how we must translate our desires into actions, and realize that, when a soul begins to mortify itself, it finds everything painful. It is painful to start giving up comforts; it is a torment to have to forego honour; even to endure a hard word may become intolerable: in short, the soul will never cease to be sorrowful, even unto death.

*   *   *   *   *   *

It is these flowers that produce fruit; these are the apple-trees of which the Bride speaks when she says: "Compass me about with apples." "Give me trials, Lord," she cries; "give me persecutions;" and she really desires them and emerges from them greatly benefited. For, as she no longer considers her own pleasure but only the giving of pleasure to God, she delights in imitating, in some degree, the most toilsome life led by Christ. . . . The Bride is quite right to make this request, for she cannot always be having enjoyment without service or suffering. I particularly notice in certain persons . . . that the farther they advance. . . the more attentive they are to the needs of their neighbours.

*   *   *   *   *   *

We must walk in poverty:
'Twas the path of God Most High
When He journey'd from the sky,
Nuns of Carmel.

He will love us all for aye;
And He calls us, day by day:
Tread we, fearless, in His way,
Nuns of Carmel.

*   *   *   *   *   *

Let us take our cross each day,
Follow Jesus as we may;
Him our Light and Him our Way
Let us follow, glad and gay,
Nuns of Carmel.

✳ JOHN ARNDT
[1555–1621]

John Arndt is said to have "declared war against verbal professions of faith." He began his classic work, *Of True Christianity*, with these words: "I have undertaken to write this piece of Practical Christianity. . . . The whole intention and design of the book is, to explain how Adam ought in us to die, and Christ again to live: it being not enough to know barely the Word of God; but if we know it, it must then be also expressed in our whole Life and Practice." Expounding this theme in the hymns and devotions he wrote, Arndt was able to turn the stream of Lutheranism toward pietism. His *Paradiesgartlein* ("little paradise") ranks along with the work of à Kempis in pietist devotion. Its verses and prayers linger upon Christ's sufferings and agonies on the cross; while the Way seems hard and frightening, Arndt contended that to live the Gospel is "sweetness, gentleness, mildness" and will "lead [the penitent Sinner] into a more pleasant and comfortable Path." In that work the following prayer occurs and indicates the tenor of his faith: "O give me Grace, that according to the Example thou hast left me, I may patiently bear my own Cross, and with a willing obedience submit to the paternal correction my heavenly Father is pleased to bestow upon me."

Pietism, with its little cells of people developing religious devotions in quiet retreat, such as the one at Herrnhut under Zinzendorf and the "colleges" of the same sort under Spener and Arndt, planted seeds on the Continent which bore fruit in England and around the world in the Wesleyan revival. The imitation theme which motivates Pietism occurs unusually strong in Arndt and recalls medieval devotion at its

116

best. "If thou believest that Christ was crucified for the sins of the world, thou must with Him be crucified the same. If thou refuseth to comply with this order, thou canst not be a living member of Christ, nor be united with Him by faith. . . . In a word: The Birth, Cross, Passion, Death, Resurrection, and Ascension of Christ, must after a spiritual manner be transacted in thee."

Of True Christianity

There are not wanting now every where such men as would be thought ministers of the Gospel and of Christ; but few are willing to be His followers also, or imitators of His holy life. At this rate, the Lord hath many ministers, but few followers! And yet is it utterly impossible for a man to be a minister and lover of Christ, unless he be also a follower of His life, according to that: If any man serve me, let him *follow* me. If a man loves Christ, he must also love to copy after His holy life, and to transcribe in his own conversation, the humility of Christ, His meekness and patience, His Cross and contempt, His reproaches and insults, though it be never so sharp and afflicting to the propensions of our natural temper. And though we are not like to express to the full that sacred pattern of the blameless life of Christ, whilst we are in this state of minority; yet it is meet that such a state should be loved, breathed after, and pursued with our utmost efforts.

* * * * * *

Thus when He taught the duty of obedience, He shewed at the same time a pattern of obedience in His own life and conduct. When He endeavoured to instil into His disciples a sense of humility, of patience, of subjection to their superiors, and of other Christian virtues; He practised them first Himself, that so His own example might have the greater influence upon the lives of others. He hath left us for this purpose, abundance of admirable instances of virtues. For being Head and Master, He thought it becoming His character to be chief also in bearing affronts, reproaches, injuries, poverty, misery, and in performing the most contemptible services, and even that of washing His disciples' feet. And thus He proved a Master, Head, and Teacher, not in doctrine only; but in life also, in example and practice.

*   *   *   *   *   *

Surely a soul, who is a sincere lover of Christ, can [do] with no other condition of life, but such as comes up nearest to the original of the blessed Life of Christ. Which conformity of our life to the life of Christ, we ought to account for our greatest gain and dignity in this world. In this, let the true lover of Christ rejoice, that he hath been thought worthy to suffer with Christ, his Head and Saviour. . . . What cause can we pretend, why we should not most willingly step over into this path of the holy Cross? Especially since we know that the Son of God Himself hath travelled this way before us, and by His holy example sanctified it, not having entered into His glory but by sufferings? And since He hath, in spite of all the insults of the enemy, entered nevertheless into glory at last . . .

*   *   *   *   *   *

In this course of our Lord's life, is not only displayed to us the abounding treasure of redemption gained by Christ, and of which He Himself is the very source and basis; but it is also most clearly demonstrated, that in this scene of sufferings, He is our great Doctor and Master, our Prophet and Shepherd, our Instructor, Light and constant Monitor; that also we, by looking unto Him, may learn to despise earthly pomp and greatness, and by closely adhering to Him, like true members of their Head, grow up into Him in all things, being rendered conformable unto His life, and rooted and grounded in His love. . . . Upon the whole: let the life of Christ be unto us a constant and awakening Monitor, to press after Him, who is the Captain of our salvation, and to die unto the world as He did. Consider the beginning, together with the progress and final conclusion of His happy life, and nothing, you'll say, speaks more loud, nothing is more evident, nothing more obvious to every one's eye, than His profound humility, wherewith He bore the contempt and reproaches of all those that love the world.

✹ JEREMY TAYLOR
[1613–1667]

Seventeenth-century England abounded in devotional books produced by writers from all the denominations which suddenly sprang up. The Anglicans produced classics all the way from Christopher Sutton's *Learn to Live* (1608) to Richard Allestree's *The Whole Duty of Man* (1658) and Robert Nelson's *The Practice of True Devotion* (1698). Better known, perhaps, are Richard Baxter's *The Saints' Everlasting Rest* and Jeremy Taylor's *Holy Living* and *Holy Dying*. One thing they all have in common: they draw heavily upon the imitation of Christ, as the subtitle of the first-mentioned work indicates: "Wherein is shewed, that the life of Christ is, and ought to be, an express pattern for imitation unto the life of a Christian, so far as in him lieth," with the title-page texts, Matthew 11:29 and John 13:15.

We forego all these devotional classics to draw upon a work by Jeremy Taylor, *The Great Exemplar*, which seems to present the most representative portrayal of the Anglican concept of imitation. Here is the accommodation of rigorous imitation to the decent life of the rational man in a cultured society. "The example of Jesus is so excellent, that it allures and tempts with its facility and sweetness . . . we find so much reason to address ourselves to a heavenly imitation of so blessed a pattern, that the reasonableness of the thing will be a great argument to chide every degree and minute of neglect." The chief virtues of the Christ-life were humility and meekness. In his *Holy Living*, he wrote: "Humility is the great ornament and jewel of Christian religion; that, whereby it is distinguished from all the wisdom of the world: it not having been taught by the wise men of the Gentiles, but first put into a discipline, and made part of a religion, by

120

our Lord Jesus Christ, who propounded himself imitable by his disciples so signally in nothing as in the twin-sisters of meekness and humility. Learn of me, for I am meek and humble; and ye shall find rest unto your souls."

An Exhortation to the Imitation of the Life of Christ

In the great council of eternity, when God set down the laws, and knit fast the eternal bands of predestination, he made it one of his great purposes to make his Son like us, that we also might be like his holy Son; he, by taking our nature; we, by imitating his holiness. 'God hath predestinated us to be conformable to the image of his Son.' (Rom. viii.29) saith the apostle. For the first in every kind is in nature propounded as the pattern of the rest. And as the sun, the prince of all the bodies of light, and the fire of all warm substances, is the principle, the rule, and the copy which they in their proportions imitate and transcribe, so is the Word incarnate the great example of all the predestinate; for 'he is the first-born among many brethren.' And therefore it was a precept of the apostle, and by his doctrine we understand its meaning, 'Put you on the Lord Jesus Christ.' (Rom. xiii. 14) The similitude declares the duty. As a garment is composed and made of the same fashion with the body, and is applied to each part in its true figure and commensuration, so should we 'put on Christ,' and imitate the whole body of his sanctity, conforming to every integral part, and express him in our lives; that God seeing our impresses, may know whose image and superscription we bear; and that we may be acknowledged for sons, when we have the air and features and resemblances of our elder brother. . . .

Secondly, I consider, that the imitation of the life of

Jesus is a duty of that excellency and perfection, that we are helped in it, not only by the assistance of a good and a great example, which possibly might be too great, and scare our endeavours and attempts; but also by its easiness, compliance and proportion to us. For Jesus in his whole life conversed with men with a modest virtue, which like a well-kindled fire fitted with just materials casts a constant heat; not like an inflamed heap of stubble, glaring with great emissions, and suddenly stooping into the thickness of smoke. His piety was even, constant, unblamable, complying with civil society, without affrightment of precedent, or prodigious instances of action greater than the imitation of men. For if we observe our blessed Saviour in the whole story of his life, although he was without sin, yet the instances of his piety were the actions of a very holy, but of an ordinary life. . . .

But now, when the example of Jesus is so excellent, that it allures and tempts with its facility and sweetness, and that we are not commanded to imitate a life, whose story tells of ecstacies in prayer, and abstractions of senses, and immaterial transportations, and fastings to the exinanition of spirits, and disabling of all animal operations; but of a life of justice and temperance, of chastity and piety, of charity and devotion; such a life without which human society cannot be conserved, and by which as our irregularities are made regular, so our weaknesses are not upbraided, nor our miseries made a mockery; we find so much reason to address ourselves to a heavenly imitation of so blessed a pattern, that the reasonableness of the thing will be a great argument to chide every degree and minute of neglect. . . .

So, when our lives are formed into the imitation of the life of the holiest Jesus, the Spirit of God returns into us, not only by the efficacy of the imitation, but by the merit and impetration of the actions of Jesus. It is reported in the Bohemian story, that St. Wenceslaus, their king, one winter night, going to his devotions in a remote church, bare-footed, in the snow and sharpness of unequal and pointed ice, his servant Podavivus, who waited upon his master's piety, and endeavoured to imitate his affections, began to faint through the violence of the snow and cold, till the king commanded him to follow him, and set his feet in the same footsteps which his feet should mark for him. The servant did so, and either fancied a cure, or found one; for he followed his prince, helped forward with shame and zeal to his imitation, and by the forming footsteps for him in the snow. In the same manner does the blessed Jesus: for since our way is trouble-some, obscure, full of objection and danger, apt to be mis-taken, and to affright our industry, he commands us to mark his footsteps, to tread where his feet have stood; and not only invites us forward by the argument of his example, but he hath trodden down much of the difficulty, and made the way easier and fit for our feet. . . .

For however Jesus had some extraordinary transvolations and acts of emigration beyond the lines of his even and ordi-nary conversation, yet it was but seldom: for his being exemplary was of so great consideration, that he chose to have fewer instances of wonder, that he might transmit the more of an imitable virtue. And therefore we may establish this for a rule and limit of our imitations; because Christ our lawgiver hath described all his Father's will in sanctions and signature of laws. Whatsoever he commanded, and what-soever he did of precise morality, or in pursuance of the laws of nature, in that we are to trace his footsteps. And in these his laws and his practice differ but as a map and a guide, a law and a judge, a rule and a precedent.

PRAYER

Holy Jesu, since thy image is imprinted on our nature by creation, let me also express thy image by all the parts of a holy life, conforming my will and affections to thy holy precepts, submitting my understanding to the dictates and lessons of perfection; imitating thy sweetness and excellencies of society, thy devotion in prayer, thy conformity to God, thy zeal tempered with meekness, thy patience heightened with charity; that heart, and hands, and eyes, and all my faculties may grow up with the increase of God, till I come to the full measure of the stature of Christ, even to be a perfect man in Christ Jesus; that at last 'in thy light I may see light,' and reap the fruits of glory from the seeds of sanctity in the imitation of thy holy life, O blessed and holy Saviour, Jesu. Amen.

✳ JAMES NAYLER
[1618–1660]

The desire to imitate Christ not only in His inward nature, but also according to His outward deeds, has led to extreme behavior on the part of certain enthusiasts. During the sudden flourishing of enthusiasm in seventeenth-century England this charge was flung around about as recklessly as the charge "radical" usually is. But there is little doubt that one James Nayler, a Quaker by inclination and association, did attempt to re-enact the life of Christ even to such particulars as His hair style and His triumphal entry into Jerusalem. This last, known as the Bristol incident, occurred when a procession composed mostly of women set out from Glastonbury with Nayler, upon his release from prison, where he had received letters actually addressed "Jesus." Enroute to Bristol the procession emulated in detail the Palm Sunday entrance of Jesus into Jerusalem. The procession immediately attracted police attention, and Nayler's arrest and subsequent trial, before Parliament itself, was projected on the charge that "he assumed the gestures, words, names and attitudes of our Lord Christ." He was found guilty and had his tongue seared.

The fact is, Nayler, before his "miscarriage" at Bristol, had much to say concerning imitation. In a tract entitled "Love to the Lost," he wrote that Jesus "humbled himself, and became obedient to the death, that he might become a living example to all Generations." Nayler insisted that "Christ is known to none but to those who receive and follow him." And perhaps the following is a cue to his extreme method of imitation: "I strive for perfection, because I find that Christ never believed less." The last note is especially true of all those who held that the Christ-powers are equally available to all men. Christ, they argued, never said, "Thou couldst not," but rather, "Thou wouldst not."

Nonetheless, most of the enthusiasts held that the true manner of imitation is that of the *spirit* behind Christ's actions, rather than the external *form* of His actions. In that sense, then, James Nayler more appropriately emulated Christ in his attitude following "restoration" to the fellowship of the Friends, after he had suffered grievous punishment and humiliation; whereupon he was able to say in the last moments of his life: "Yet I have felt a spirit which delights in forgiving debts, and seeks all occasion thereto, even where it is not sought, but seeks; and by this spirit I have been able to bear all things while it is with me, else had I not been at this day." Nayler's full comments on this "spirit" which he borrowed from Christ have been woven into twenty-six lovely and love-provoking sonnets by Kenneth Boulding, an American professor of economics.

Quaker imitation has always held, after Francis Howgill, that "the Life of Christ must be felt within, enjoyed and possessed within . . ." This Christ within is to be followed in terms of the simple, humble, lowly, and persecuted Jesus of history. Otherwise it is a "lifeless imitation," to use their term. George Fox said, "Christ is an example to all who walk after; and if thou knew'st what an example is, thou wouldst know what a figure is, to come up to Christ's same fulness." Isaac Penington spoke of Christ's humility and recorded that "Christ urgeth this upon his disciples from his own pattern. . . . And this is the pattern which all his disciples are to walk by." In the century those who so believed did not have to look for trouble; they encountered persecution on every hand. In one of the more famous replies to their persecutors, in the form of a printed public statement, they confessed that "these poor Creatures know how their Master fared, and rejoyce to suffer with him, by whom alone they hope to be glorified . . . and yet a necessity lies upon us (if we will be the Lord's Disciples) to take up our cross daily and follow him . . ."

THERE IS A SPIRIT WHICH I FEEL

There is a spirit which I feel that delights to do no evil, nor to revenge any wrong, but delights to endure all things, in hope to enjoy its own in the end. Its hope is to outlive all wrath and contention, and to weary out all exaltation and cruelty, or whatever is of a nature contrary to itself. It sees to the end of all temptations. As it bears no evil in itself, so it conceives none in thoughts to any other. If it be betrayed, it bears it, for its ground and spring is the mercies and forgiveness of God. Its crown is meekness, its life is everlasting love unfeigned; and takes its kingdom with entreaty and not with contention, and keeps it by lowliness of mind. In God alone it can rejoice, though none else regard it, or can own its life. It's conceived in sorrow, and brought forth without any to pity it, nor doth it murmur at grief and oppression. It never rejoiceth but through sufferings: for with the world's joy it is murdered. I found it alone, being forsaken. I have fellowship therein with them who lived in dens and desolate places in the earth, who through death obtained this resurrection and eternal holy life.

✱ WILLIAM PENN
[1644–1718]

Forsaking the prominence of his father's estate and church affiliation, when both were at a premium in this period of England's social and religious ferment, William Penn became a Friend at the age of twenty-two. Two years later, he was thrown into prison for his beliefs; and *No Cross, No Crown*, like so many other great Christian books, was born in the agonies and solitude of the cell. John Bunyan, the Baptist whose classic *Pilgrim's Progress* was likewise born in a cell and who knew the inside of England's prisons as well as any Quaker, has given voice to the experience of many who were persecuted for their religious convictions:

> God sometimes visits prisoners more
> > Than lordly palaces,
> He often knocketh at the door,
> > When he their houses miss.

> * * * * * *

> This gaol to us is as a hill,
> > From whence we plainly see
> Beyond this world, and take our fill
> > Of things that lasting be.

No Cross, No Crown emerged at once as a general apology for Quakerism in behalf of its practice, as Robert Barclay's *Apology* pertained to its theory. As much as any book, *No Cross, No Crown* supports a contemporary opinion that "these people are somewhat of a softer temper, and seem to recommend Christianity by the charm of its love, mercy, and goodness, rather than by the terrors of its judgments . . ."

The book went through many editions even during the

lifetime of Penn, and its real purpose is stated by him in a preface to a later edition: "Christ's cross is Christ's way to Christ's crown. This is the subject of the following discourse; first written during my confinement in the Tower of London, in the year 1668; now reprinted with great enlargement of matter and testimonies; that thou mayest be won to Christ; or if won already, brought nearer to him. It is a path, which God in his everlasting kindness guided my feet into, in the flower of my youth. He took me by the hand, and led me out of the pleasures, vanities, and hopes of the world. I have tasted Christ's judgments, and of his mercies, and of the world's frowns and reproaches. I rejoice in my experience, and dedicate it to thy service in Christ."

This is the life of the blessed cross of Christ, which is the subject of the following discourse, and what thou, O man, must take up, if thou intendest to be the disciple of Jesus. Nor canst thou be said to receive Christ, or believe in him, whilst thou rejectest his cross. For as receiving Christ is the means appointed of God to salvation, so bearing the daily cross after him is the only true testimony of receiving him; and therefore it is enjoined by him, as the great token of discipleship, "If any man will come after me, let him deny himself, and take up his cross, and follow me."

This, Christendom, is what thou hast so much wanted, and the want of it has proved the cause of thy miserable declension from pure Christianity.

*　*　*　*　*　*

. . . we must either renounce the belief of what the Lord Jesus hath told us, "That whosoever doth not take up his daily cross, and come after him, cannot be his disciple;"

or, admitting it for truth, conclude, that the generality of Christendom do miserably deceive and disappoint themselves in the great business of Christianity, and their own salvation.

*   *   *   *   *   *

What is the great work and business of the cross respecting man?

This indeed is of such mighty moment to be truly, plainly and thoroughly answered, that all that went before seems only to serve as a preface to it; and miscarrying in this, to be no less than a misguidance of the soul about its way to blessedness. I shall therefore pursue the question, with God's help, and the best knowledge he hath given me, in the experience of several years' discipleship.

The great work and business of the cross of Christ in man, is self-denial; a word of much depth in itself, and of sore contradiction to the world; little understood; but less embraced by it; which yet must be borne. The Son of God is gone before us, and, by the bitter cup he drank, and the baptism he suffered, has left us an example that we should follow his steps. This made him put that hard question to the wife of Zebedee and her two sons, upon her soliciting that one might sit at his right, and the other at his left hand in his kingdom. "Are ye able to drink of the cup that I shall drink of, and to be baptised with the baptism I am baptised with?" It seems their faith was strong; they answered, "We are able." Upon which he replied, "Ye shall drink indeed of my cup, and be baptised with the baptism I am baptised with;" but their reward he left to his Father.

What was the cup he drank, and baptism he suffered? I answer; they were the denial and offering up of himself by the eternal Spirit to the will of God, undergoing the tribulations of his life, and agonies of his death upon the cross, for man's salvation.

What is our cup and cross that we should drink and suffer? They are the denying and offering up of ourselves, by the same spirit, to do or suffer the will of God for his service and glory. This is the true life and obedience of the cross of Jesus; narrow still, but before, an unbeaten way. When there was none to help, not one to open the seals, to give knowledge, or to direct the course of poor man's recovery, he came in the greatness of his love and strength; and though clothed with the infirmities of a mortal man, being within fortified by the Almightiness of an immortal God, he travelled through all the straits and difficulties of humanity; and, first of all others trod the untrodden path to blessedness.

O come, let us follow him, the most unwearied, the most victorious captain of our salvation! to whom all the great Alexanders and mighty Caesars of the world are less than the poorest soldier of their camps could be to them. They were all great princes of their kind, and conquerors too, but on very differing principles. Christ made himself of no reputation to save mankind; but these plentifully ruined people, to augment theirs. They vanquished others, not themselves. Christ conquered self, which always vanquished them. Of merit therefore, he is the most excellent prince and conqueror. Besides, they advanced their empire by rapine and blood, he by suffering and persuasion; he never by compulsion, they always by force prevailed. Misery and slavery followed all their victories; his, brought greater freedom and felicity to those he overcame. In all they did, they sought to please themselves; in all he did, he aimed to please his Father, who is God of gods, King of kings, and Lord of lords.

It is this most perfect pattern of self-denial we must follow, if ever we will come to glory.

*   *   *   *   *   *

If none can be true disciples, but they that come to bear the daily cross, and none bear the cross, but those who follow the example of the Lord Jesus Christ, through his baptism, and afflictions and temptations; and none are so baptized with him, but those whose minds are retired from the vanities in which the generality of the world live, and become obedient to the holy light and divine grace, with which they have been enlightened from on high, and thereby are daily exercised to the crucifying of every contrary affection, and bringing immortality to light; if none are true disciples, but such, as most undoubtedly they are not, then let the people of these days soberly reflect upon themselves, and they will conclude, that none who live and delight in these vain customs, and this unchristlike conversation, can be true Christians, or disciples of the crucified Jesus. For otherwise, how would it be a cross, or the Christian life, matter of difficulty and reproach? No, the offense of the cross would soon cease, which is the power of God to them that believe; that every lust and vanity may be subdued, and the creature brought into an holy subjection of mind to the heavenly will of its Creator. For therefore has it been said, that Jesus Christ was and is manifested, that by his holy, self-denying life and doctrine, he might put a baffle upon the proud minds of men, and by the immortality he brought, and daily brings, to light, might stain the glory of their fading rests and pleasures; that having their minds weaned from them, and being crucified thereunto, they might seek another country, and obtain an everlasting inheritance.

✳ FRANÇOIS FÉNELON
[1651–1715]

The quietistic movement among the Catholics in France developed into a "fashionable" experience for the well-to-do. As tutor to the grandsons of Louis XIV, Fénelon had access to the court life of the time, which was profligate and distrustful. However, he held spiritual conferences with a small number of earnest people who sought a deeper spiritual life, and the work known as *Christian Perfection* grew out of these sessions. We might confess that if Fénelon felt that true Christian living could sprout then and there, considering the Court of Louis XIV, we have some encouragement for our own times. Fénelon not only felt that, but he even set before these worldly persons Christianity in terms of imitation and cross-bearing. "To be Christians is to be imitators of Jesus Christ. In what can we imitate him except in his humiliations?" In a chapter on the value and uses of crosses, there occurs the following prayer, one of his many deeply moving prayers for spirituality: "Make us fix our eyes constantly . . . upon Jesus thy Son who is our model in all suffering. Thou hast nailed him to the cross for us. Thou hast made him the man of sorrows to teach us how useful sorrows are. Let weak and timid human nature be still then at the sight of Jesus covered with shame and crushed by suffering."

The Sacred Heart school of French mysticism which followed Fénelon developed under Berulle what is known as "internal imitation." They stressed imitation which emerges from meditation upon the Passion of Christ. "Thus it is with the virtues; there is a dye hidden in the Heart of Jesus, and when a soul plunges therein in love, adoration

and all the other duties of worship, it will readily assume
this tint."

Imitation of Jesus Christ

We must imitate Jesus. This is to live as he lived, to
think as he thought, to conform ourselves to his image,
which is the seal of our sanctification.

What a difference of behaviour! The nothing believes itself
something; and the All-Powerful makes himself nothing. I
make myself nothing with thee, Lord. I make thee the
entire sacrifice of my pride, of the vanity which possesses
me up to the present. Help my good intention. Keep from
me the occasions of my falling. "Turn my eyes that I see
not vanity," that I see only thee, and that I see myself
before thee. It will be then that I shall know what I am
and what thou art.

Jesus Christ is born in a stable. He has to flee into
Egypt. He passes thirty years of his life in the shop of a
craftsman. He suffers hunger, thirst, weariness. He is poor,
scorned and abject. He teaches the doctrine of heaven, and
no one listens to him. All the great and the wise pursue
him, take him, and make him suffer frightful torments.
They treat him like a slave, make him die between two
thieves, after having preferred a thief to him. That was the
life that Jesus Christ chose, and we, we have a horror of
every sort of humiliation! The slightest contempt is un-
bearable to us.

Let us compare our life to that of Jesus Christ. Let us
remember that he is the master, and that we are the slaves;
that he is all-powerful, and that we are only weakness. He

lowers himself, and we raise ourselves. Let us accustom ourselves to think so often of our wretchedness, that we may have only contempt for ourselves. Can we with justice feel contempt for others and dwell on their faults, when we are full of them ourselves? Let us commence to walk on the road which Jesus Christ has marked for us, since it is the only one which can lead us to him.

And how can we find Jesus Christ, if we do not seek him in the conditions of his mortal life, that is to say, in solitude, in silence, in poverty and suffering, in persecutions and contumelies, in the cross and in annihilations? The saints find him in heaven, in the splendour of glory and in ineffable joy, but it is after having lived with him on earth in shame, suffering and humiliation. To be Christians is to be imitators of Jesus Christ. In what can we imitate him except in his humiliations? Nothing else can draw us to him. As all-powerful, we ought to adore him; as just, we ought to fear him; as good and merciful, we ought to love him with all our strength; as humble, submissive, lowly and faithful unto death, we ought to imitate him.

Let us not pretend to be able to reach this state by our own strength. Everything in us resists it. But let us console ourselves in the presence of God. Jesus Christ has wanted to feel all our weaknesses. He is a compassionate pontiff, who has wanted to be tempted as we are. Let us then find all our strength in him who became voluntarily weak to strengthen us. Let us enrich ourselves by his poverty, and let us say with confidence, "I can do all things in him who strengthens me."

I want to follow, O Jesus, the road which thou hast taken! I want to imitate thee; I only can do so by thy grace. O Saviour, lowly and humble, give me the knowledge of true Christians and a feeling of contempt for myself. And may I learn the lesson which is incomprehensible to the human spirit, which is to die to self by mortification and true humility.

# WILLIAM LAW

[1686–1761]

Law is known primarily for the pen-portraits in A Serious
Call to a Devout and Holy Life, which exposed nominal
Christians of his day. These nominal Christians are the sort
with us to this day, such as Miss Do-Gooder, so very active
in the Missionary Society for the Poor Africans, but who
mistreats her housemaid whose forebears are recently from
there; and Mr. Skinflint, so eager to leave a sizeable endow-
ment for the church that he contributes a quarter a Sunday.
However, Law's book A Treatise of Christian Perfection
contains the wealth of his spiritual wisdom. Its theme is the
core of Law's conception of imitation: "For we may as well
expect to go to a heaven where Christ is not, as to go to
that where He is, without the Spirit and Temper which
carried Him thither."

This important English mystic remained a staunch member of the Church of England, but drew heavily upon the
mystic writer Boehme. We would expect him to emphasize
imitation of Christ in terms of internal conformity. He did;
but living in a worldly and rationalistic age, he nonetheless
stressed imitation in the common life of the people. We
must fulfill our common life vocation as Christ fulfilled His
divine vocation. "If we are to follow Christ, it must be in
our common way of spending every day." Especially in the
Christ-virtues, suffering and humility, can all Christians
participate in God's continuous redemptive process. "If a
man in one instance can act disinterestedly, and solely from
this principle that from his heart he embraces Christ as
his suffering Lord and pattern, he helps to kindle the
heavenly life within the soul."

Besides his writings, Law is known for the establishment of almshouses and schools for the poor in his native village, never forgetting to identify himself with the needy neighbor as Christ had done.

All Christians are required to imitate the Life and Example of Jesus Christ.

Since therefore it is the great end of our religion to make us fellow-heirs with Christ, and partakers of the same happiness, it is not to be wondered at that our religion should require us to be like Christ in this life, to imitate his example, that we may enter into that state of happiness which he enjoys in the kingdom of heaven.

For how can we think that we are going to the blessed Jesus, that we are to be hereafter as he is, unless we conform to his spirit in this life, and make it our great endeavour to be what he was when he was here. Let it therefore here be observed, that the nature of our religion teaches us this duty in a more convincing manner, than any particular precepts concerning it. For the most ordinary understanding must feel the force and reasonableness of this argument. You are born to depart out of this world, to ascend to that state of bliss, to live in such enjoyment of God to all eternity, as our blessed Saviour now enjoys; you are therefore to live in the spirit and temper that he lived, and make yourself first like him here, that you may be like him hereafter. So that we need not look for particular texts of Scripture which command us to imitate the life of Christ, because we are taught this duty by a stronger and more convincing authority; because, as the end and design of our

religion is to make us one with Christ hereafter, partakers of
the same state of life, so it plainly calls us to be one with
him here, and to be partakers of that same spirit and temper
in which he lived on earth. When it is said, that we are to
imitate the life of Christ, it is not meant that we are called
to the same manner of life, or the same sort of actions,
for this cannot be; but it is certain that we are called to
the same spirit and temper, which was the spirit and temper
of our blessed Saviour's life and actions. We are to be
like him in heart and mind, to act by the same rule, to
look towards the same end, and to govern our lives by the
same spirit. This is an imitation of Jesus Christ, which is as
necessary to salvation as it is necessary to believe in his
name. This is the sole end of all the counsels, commands,
and doctrines of Christ, to make us like himself, to fill us
with his spirit and temper, and makes us live according to
the rule and manner of his life. As no doctrines are true,
but such as are according to the doctrines of Christ, so it is
equally certain, that no life is regular or Christian, but such
as is according to the pattern and example of the life of
Christ. For he lived as infallibly as he taught; and it is as
irregular to vary from his example, as it is false to dissent
from his doctrines.

*   *   *   *   *   *

. . . these differences [between us and Christ] do not
make the life of Christ to be less the rule and model of all
Christians. For as I observed before, it is the spirit and
temper of Christ, that all Christians are to imitate, and not
his particular actions; they are to do their proper work in
that spirit and temper in which Christ did the work on
which he was sent. So that although Christians are not
redeemers of the world, as he was, though they have not
his extraordinary powers, nor that great work to finish which

he had, yet they have their work to do in the manner that he did his . . .

*   *   *   *   *   *

For no circumstances of life can hinder us from being examples of piety and goodness, and making our lives a lesson of instruction to all that are about us. And he that lives an exemplary life, though his state be ever so poor and mean, is largely contributing to the salvation of others, and proving himself the best follower of his Lord and Master. . . . Let us therefore not vainly say that if we had lived in our Saviour's days, we would have followed him, or that if we could work miracles, we would devote ourselves to his glory. For to follow Christ as far as we can in our present state, and to do all that we are able for his glory, is as acceptable to him, as if we were working miracles in his name.

*   *   *   *   *   *

For besides, that there is the same authority in all that our Saviour did, which obliges us to conform to his whole example: can any one tell why we should have more value for this world than our Saviour had?

*   *   *   *   *   *

Again, *learn of me,* (saith our blessed Saviour) *for I am meek and lowly of Heart.* . . . Let us not therefore deceive ourselves; let us not fancy that we are truly humble, though living in all the *pride* and *splendour* of Life; let us not imagine that we have any power to render ourselves humble and lowly any other way than by an humble and lowly course of life. Christ is our *pattern* and *example;* he was content to be *one person;* he did not pretend to *impossibilities;* to reconcile the *pride* of life with the *lowliness* of religion; but renounced the one, that he might be a true example of the other.

. . . We must therefore make it the great business and aim of our lives, to be like Christ; and this not in a loose or general way, but with great nicety and exactness, always looking to his Spirit, to his ends and designs, to his tempers, to his ways and conversation in the world, as the exact model and Rule of our lives.

JOHN WESLEY
[1703–1791]

CHARLES WESLEY
[1707–1788]

In the early period of John Wesley's life the works of à Kempis, Taylor, and Law greatly influenced him. In 1735, at 31, he published his own edition of à Kempis' work, entitled *The Christian's Pattern*—"an independent translation from the original Latin." The Wesley Preface is built around the idea that "the whole Treatise on the Imitation of Christ is a complete and finished work, comprehending all that related to Christian perfection . . . (It expounds) the essence of Christian perfection, the ways and degrees by which it is attained and the means or instruments of it." Wesley substantiated the historical rootage of the concept by citing fifteen passages from the Gospels and the Epistles and two from the Fathers (from Augustine and Bernard). He concluded the Preface with the admonition, "Labor to work yourself up into a temper correspondent with what you have read."

The historian G. C. Cell, commenting on Wesley's development, claims that this view is valid only for his "pre-evangelical period," 1725-1738. However, perfection is defined in his later work "A Plain Account of Christian Perfection" as "the resemblance of God who is the first and supreme excellency, and the imitation of Christ who is the effulgence of his glory, the most perfect pattern of all holiness." While he may have forsaken the monastic implications of à Kempis, his contact with the Moravians both on his missionary trip to Georgia and afterward in London and Herrnhut must have confirmed him in his interpretation of imitation.

Charles especially stressed the imitation of Christ. He wrote a long series of hymns, which were never widely circulated, entitled "The Trial of Faith," to set forth what imitation means. While these first hymns echoed medieval attention upon the Passion of Christ, Charles came to see that imitation entailed attention to the other deeds of Jesus' life as well as to the contemporary Christ. The idea is expressed nobly in his great hymn, "Holy Lamb, Who Thee Confess."

These hymns and *The Christian Library*, in which series *The Christian's Pattern* appeared, were devised by the brothers for the methodical discipline of the religious development which gave Methodists their name.

HOLY LAMB, WHO THEE CONFESS

Holy Lamb, who Thee confess,
Followers of Thy holiness,
Thee they ever keep in view,
Ever ask, "What shall we do?"
Govern'd by Thy only will,
All Thy words we would fulfill,
Would in all Thy footsteps go,
Walk as Jesus walk'd below.

While Thou didst on earth appear,
Servant to Thy servants here,
Mindful of Thy place above,
All Thy life was prayer and love.
Such our whole employment be,
Works of faith and charity;
Works of love on man bestow'd,
Secret intercourse with God.

Early in the temple met,
Let us still our Saviour greet;
Nightly to the mount repair,
Join our praying Pattern there.
There by wrestling faith obtain
Power to work for God again;
Power His Image to retrieve,
Power, like Thee, our Lord, to live.

Vessels, instruments of grace,
Pass we thus our happy days
'Twixt the mount and multitude,
Doing or receiving good;
Glad to pray and labour on,
Till our earthly course is run,
Till we, on the sacred tree,
Bow the head and die like Thee.

* * * * * *

CHRIST OUR PATTERN

Pardon, and grace, and heaven, to buy,
　My bleeding *Sacrifice* expired;
But didst Thou not my *Pattern* die,
　That, by Thy glorious Spirit fired,
Faithful to death I might endure,
And make the crown by suffering sure?

Thou didst the meek example leave,
　That I might in Thy footsteps tread;
Might, like the Man of Sorrows, grieve,
　And groan, and bow with Thee my head;
Thy dying in my body bear,
And all Thy state of suffering share.

JONATHAN EDWARDS
[1703–1758]

So prevalent is the popular appraisal of Edwards in the light of his revivalistic sermon "Sinners in the Hands of an angry God" among puritanic New Englanders, that it may be a surprise to many readers that his name should appear in this procession. The accompanying extract, however, is just as much an integral part of Edwards' thinking, since it comes from his mature and profound work on ethics, "A Treatise on Religious Affections." In the introduction he admitted that his efforts as a revivalist in the religious awakening of New England were in danger of misinterpretation. "It is by mixing counterfeit with true religion, that the devil has always gained the greatest advantage against the cause of Christ." Then, with the best philosophic mind of the time, he set forth a conception of the converted man as one who develops the virtue of "disinterested benevolence" by "the most vigorous and sensible exercises of the inclination and will of the soul." While he argued openly to keep the balance between the righteousness which is a gift of Christ and the works which a Christian must do, he nowhere stated the case better than in the following: "Thus, if a man appears to imitate Christ, and greatly to exert himself to promote his kingdom and interest in the world, we are taught by rational principles, that this is an evidence of love, more to be depended upon than if he only talked of his love to Christ, and related, what he might call, his experience of the love of Christ."

It is clear from the last paragraph of the accompanying excerpt that what he said in his introduction was carefully weighed: "The consideration of these things has long en-

145

gaged my serious attention." He wished to make clear that
professing Christians have no easy salvation, as many were
apparently interpreting the evangelistic message. " 'Strait'
indeed 'is the gate, and narrow' indeed 'is the way, that
leads to life, and few there be that find it.' "

Religious Affections

But yet it is evident, that religion consists so much in
the affections, that without holy affection there is no religion. . . . All the virtues of the Lamb of God, his humility, his patience, his meekness, his submission, his obedience, his love, and his compassion, are presented to our
contemplation in a manner the most adapted to move our
affections. . . . If we judge of the nature of Christianity by
the word of God, this spirit and temper must be regarded as
forming the true and distinguishing disposition of all real
Christians; it is the spirit by which they are so governed
that they take from it their proper character and denomina-
tion. . . .

. . . There are some virtues which, in a peculiar manner,
agree with the nature and design of the Gospel constitution,
and which were more particularly exercised by Jesus Christ
in the work of redemption. These virtues are such as humility,
meekness, mercy, forgiveness, and love; they therefore belong,
in a very special manner, to the Christian character.

These virtues are represented as forming the character of
Christ himself, the great Head of the Christian church . . .

. . . And as these virtues are especially characteristic of
Christ, so they are also characteristic of Christians. Christians
are Christlike. None deserve to bear the name who do not

exhibit the likeness of Christ: the new man is renewed after the image of him that creates him. (Colossians 3:10.) The elect were predestinated to be conformed to the image of the Son of God, that he might be the firstborn among many brethren. (Romans 8:29.) Christ is full of grace, and all Christians receive of his fullness grace for grace: there is grace in Christians answering to grace in Christ, such a correspondence as there is between the wax and the seal, the same kind of graces, and such a spirit and temper. Christians who shine by reflecting the light of the Sun of Righteousness, shine with the same kind of brightness, the same mild, benignant beams. Those lamps of the spiritual temple which are kindled by fire from heaven, burn with the same kind of flame. It would be strange if Christians were not of the same temper and spirit as Christ, when they live so that it is not they that live, but Christ that liveth in them. A Christian spirit is the mark which Christ sets upon the souls of his people: his seal in their foreheads, bearing his image and superscription. Christians are followers, or imitators of Christ; and they are so in proportion as they learn of him, who is meek and lowly of heart. True Christians are distinguished by the meek and loving temper of Christ; for as many as are in Christ, have put on Christ. (Romans 13:14.) The church is not only clothed with his righteousness, but also adorned with his graces.

* * * * * *

Mere pretenders to religion will not endure the trials to which, in general, professors are exposed; they will not continue faithful to Christ in practice, and follow him whithersoever he goes. Herein principally consists the straitness of the gate, and the narrowness of the way that leads to life—the way of life is a way of self-denial and self-renunciation. From what has been said, it is manifest that

Christian practice, or a holy life, is a great and distinguishing evidence of saving grace.

*   *   *   *   *   *

Thus, if a man appears to imitate Christ, and greatly to exert himself to promote his kingdom and interest in the world, we are taught by rational principles, that this is an evidence of love, more to be depended upon than if he only talked of his love to Christ, and related, what he might call, his experience of the love of Christ.

*   *   *   *   *   *

Hence it also appears, that in what has been said of the importance of holy practice, as the most decisive mark of sincerity, there is nothing legal: nothing derogatory to the freedom and sovereignty of Gospel grace; nothing in the least clashing with the Gospel doctrine of justification by faith alone, without the works of the law; nothing in the least tending to lessen the glory of the Mediator, and our dependence on his righteousness; nothing infringing on the special prerogatives of faith, in the affair of salvation; nothing in any way detracting from the glory of God, and of his mercy; nothing tending to exalt man, or to lessen his dependence and obligations.

Anabaptist Swiss Brethren
[1715 and 1527]

Radical Christianity in terms of imitation of Christ has ever been characteristic of the Anabaptists whether expressed in the *Confession of Faith* formulated by Peter Rideman the Hutterian in 1565, or in the works of those following Menno Simons, who gathered the scattered Anabaptists of the Reformation into a peaceful, evangelical community. Each group was to be controlled by the spirit of the Sermon on the Mount; they were to fulfill in their daily habits the life of Christ (which entailed no oaths, no swords, no political participation); and they were to live in community of goods, in filial equality, and in separation from the rest of the world.

Ein Send-Brief, An Epistle by a Lover of God's Word, written by an anonymous Mennonite from a prison in Berne, Switzerland, became for subsequent believers a standard devotional book, and for that reason merits our attention. It insists throughout that the brethren must be willing to suffer like Christ, since suffering is understood as the inevitable consequence of the fully obedient life. "Whoever would follow Christ, must follow him in a suffering manner," is its theme. This is in the true Anabaptist mood, for as early as 1535 Hans Haffner had written: "The world accepts Christ quite readily as a gift, but from the point of view of suffering does not know Him at all."

Mennonite piety, as distinct from Lutheran piety under Spener and Catholic piety of the Sacred Heart variety, did not result in a mood of passive enjoyment of what Christ has done for us, but rather it issued in an active reincarnation of the life Christ lived. For it the Following of Christ has

149

two meanings: love and cross. "Cross" stands for the suffering that results from the clash with the world which despises the Christian, and "love" stands for the complete renunciation of force and for full brotherly sharing. While *Ein Send-Brief* is little more than a paraphrase of the Scriptures emphasizing *imitatio*, cross-bearing and love, the two sections here quoted are original.

Ein Send-Brief

AN EXHORTATION ON THE FOLLOWING OF CHRIST

O Thou sweet loving Friend, the Lord Jesus Christ, Thou tender, humiliated, patient Heart, what a splendid example of the holy life Thou hast left us, that we should follow in Thy footsteps. Thou art the unspotted mirror of all virtue, the perfect example of holiness, the blameless rule of piety, the certain standard of justice. O! how different is my sinful life compared with Thy holy Life. I ought to live in Thee as a new creature, but I live more in the old creature, namely in Adam, than in Thee, my dear Lord Jesus Christ; I ought to live according to the spirit, but sorrowfully I live according to the flesh—though I know what the Scriptures say: "Whoever lives according to the flesh, dies by the flesh." O! Thou friendly, patient, longsuffering Heart, forgive me my sins, cover my transgressions, overlook my misdeeds, turn Thy holy, pure eyes from my impurity, do not cast me from Thy countenance, do not reject me from Thy house as something impure and undesirable, purge from my heart all pride—the weed of the devil—, and plant in me Thy humility as the root and fundamental of virtue, and destroy the source of all desire of vengeance, and grant me Thy noble tenderness.

O Thou gracious ornament of all virtue, glorify my heart with pure belief, with fiery love, living hope, holy devotion, childlike fear. O Thou, my only Refuge! my love and my hope, my honor, my glory, Thy life was nothing other than love, tenderness, and compassion; therefore let Thy noble Life also be in me, Thy virtuous Life also be my life. Let my spirit, body and soul be in Thee, so that I may live in Thee, and Thee in me. Let me live in Thee and not in myself alone; let me, therefore, recognize Thee and have love for Thee, that I may walk the same way Thou hast walked.

If Thou art my Light, then shine in me; if Thou art my Life, then live in me; if Thou art my Glory, then glorify me graciously; if Thou art my Joy, then rejoice in me; if I am Thy dwelling, then possess me alone; let me be Thy tool, that my life, my soul, and my spirit, may be holy.

Thou Eternal Way, accompany me; Thou Eternal Truth, teach me; Thou Eternal Life, refresh me. Let me not be the tool of the evil one, that he may fulfill and practice in me his evil, lying, pride, greed, anger and uncleanliness; for that is the image of satan from which Thou wouldst save me, O Thou Lovely and Perfect Image of God. Renew my body, spirit and soul daily according to Thine image until I am perfected. Let me reject the world, so that I may live in Thee; let me ascend with Thee that I may go with Thee to heaven; let me be crucified with Thee that I may enter into Thy Kingdom.

Amen.

*   *   *   *   *   *

A HYMN ON THE FOLLOWING
OF JESUS CHRIST

Follow me, speaks Christ our Hero,
  Follow me, you Christians all;
Deny yourselves, shun the world,
  Follow My voice with rejoicing,
Take up your Cross and tribulations
  And follow in My footsteps—
  And follow in My footsteps.

I am the Light, I illuminate for you
  The Holy virtuous life;
Whoever comes to me, and follows me,
  Dares not hover in the darkness:
I am the Way, and I know well
  How one should truly walk before God—
  How one should truly walk before God.

My Heart is full of humbleness,
  Full of love is my soul;
My Mouth overflows forever
  With sweet oil of tenderness:
My spirit, temper, strength, and thought
  All is God-given—it behold—
  All is God-given—it behold.

*   *   *   *   *   *

So let us, then, the dear Christ
  Follow with full soul and spirit,
And joyously, with faith and cheer
  Stand by Him in suffering:
For who does not fight, will not
  Carry the crown of eternal life—
  Carry the crown of eternal life.
                        Amen.

*   *   *   *   *   *

Schleitheim Confession of Faith

In the perfection of Christ, however, only the ban is used for a warning and for the excommunication of the one who has sinned, without putting the flesh to death— simply the warning and the command to sin no more.

Now it will be asked by many who do not recognize [this as] the will of Christ for us, whether a Christian may or should employ the sword against the wicked for the defense and protection of the good, or for the sake of love.

Our reply is unanimously as follows: Christ teaches and commands us to learn of Him, for He is meek and lowly in heart and so shall we find rest to our souls. Also Christ says to the heathenish woman who was taken in adultery, not that one should stone her according to the law of His Father (and yet He says, As the Father has commanded me, thus I do), but in mercy and forgiveness and warning, to sin no more. Such [an attitude] we also ought to take completely according to the rule of the ban.

Secondly, it will be asked concerning the sword, whether a Christian shall pass sentence in worldly dispute and strife such as unbelievers have with one another. This is our united answer: Christ did not wish to decide or pass judgment between brother and brother in the case of the inheritance, but refused to do so. Therefore we should do likewise.

Thirdly, it will be asked concerning the sword, Shall one be a magistrate if one should be chosen as such? The answer is as follows: They wished to make Christ king, but He fled and did not view it as the arrangement of His Father. Thus shall we do as He did, and follow Him, and so shall we not walk in darkness. For He Himself says, He who wishes to come after me, let him deny himself and take up his cross and follow me. Also, He Himself forbids the [employment of] the force of the sword saying, The worldly princes lord it over them, etc., but not so shall it be with you. Further, Paul says, Whom God did foreknow He also did predestinate to be conformed to the image of His Son, etc. Also Peter says, Christ has suffered (not ruled) and left us an example, that ye should follow His steps.

✴ JOHN WOOLMAN
[1720–1772]

"If I were asked to date the birth of social conscience in its present-day form," writes Dean Willard L. Sperry, "I think I should put it on the twenty-sixth day of the eighth month of the year 1758—the day John Woolman in a public meeting verbally denounced Negro slavery." Like his predecessors in the British Isles, Woolman was to arouse the complacent churchmen of America to a new area for the expansion of Christianity. The earlier Friends had insisted upon the reality of the inner man in everyday affairs, upon developing the Light Within. Woolman, while building upon this foundation, pioneered on the frontiers of social compassion. In a new country caught in the throes of economic greed and acquisitiveness, he called people to simple Christian living and to social sensitivity.

His *Journal* stands with the classics of spiritual insight in that it reveals the heart of a devout man and his times. One mood he seems to have learned from his association with Christ, and he seems to be ever searching for some new way to express it: "I have found a deep Fellow-feeling"; "There is a Love clothes my Mind"; "Compassion hath filled my Heart toward my Fellow Creature"; "I have been drawn by a Sympathizing tenderness." These are some of the peculiar phrases he employs.

In a tract usually appended to his *Journal*, "Considerations on the True Harmony of Mankind," Woolman inadvertently disclosed how much his own mind had conformed to Christ's: "As my Mind hath been brought into a Brotherly Feeling with the Poor, as to the Things of this Life, who are under Trials in regard to getting a living in a Way answerable to the Purity of Truth; a Labour of Heart hath attended me, that their Way may not be made difficult through the Love of Money in those who are tried with plentiful Estates, but that they with Tenderness of Heart may sympathize with them." Woolman may be called one of the earliest exponents of "one world" and classless society from a Christian point of view.

On the Example of Christ

Jesus Christ, in promoting the Happiness of others, was not deficient in looking for the Helpless, who lay in Obscurity, nor did he save any Thing to render himself honourable amongst Men, which might have been of more Use to the weak Members in his Father's Family; of whose Compassion towards us I may now speak a little. He who was perfectly happy in himself, moved with infinite Love, took not upon him the Nature of Angels, but our imperfect Natures, and therein wrestled with the Temptations which attend us in this Life; and being the Son of him who is greater than Earthly Princes, yet became a Companion to poor, sincere-hearted Men; and though he gave the clearest Evidence that Divine Power attended him, yet the most unfavourable Constructions were framed by a self-righteous People; those Miracles represented as the Effect of a diabolical Power, and Endeavours used to render him hateful, as having his Mission from the Prince of Darkness; nor did their Envy cease till they took him like a Criminal, and brought him to Trial. Though some may affect to carry the Appearance of being unmoved at the Apprehension of Distress, our dear Redeemer, who was perfectly sincere, having the same human Nature which we have, and feeling, a little before he was apprehended, the Weight of that Work upon him, for which he came into the World, was *sorrowful even unto Death*; here the human Nature struggled to be excused from a Cup so bitter; but his Prayers centered in Resignation, *Not my Will but thine be done*. In this Conflict, so great was his Agony that *Sweat like Drops of Blood fell from him to the Ground.*

* * * * * *

Now this Mind being in us, which was in Christ Jesus, it removes from our Hearts the Desire of Superiority, Worldly Honour, or Greatness; a deep Attention is felt to the Divine Counsellor, and an ardent Engagement to promote, as far as we may be enabled, the Happiness of Mankind universally: This State, where every Motion from a selfish Spirit yieldeth to pure Love, I may, with Gratitude to the Father of Mercies acknowledge, is often opened before me as a Pearl to dig after; attended with a living Concern, that amongst the many Nations and Families on the Earth, those who believe in the Messiah, that *he was manifested to destroy the Works of the Devil, and thus to take away the Sins of the World*, may experience the Will of our Heavenly Father, *may be done on Earth as it is in Heaven*. Strong are the Desires I often feel, that this Holy Profession may remain unpolluted, and the Believers in Christ may so abide in the pure inward Feeling of his Spirit, that the Wisdom from above may shine forth in their Living, as a Light by which others may be instrumentally helped on their Way, in the true harmonious Walking.

SOREN KIERKEGAARD

[1813–1855]

"The 'imitation' must be introduced, but *without authority*, that is and remains my category." Thus, under the compulsion of grace, did this last century Danish "contemporary with Christ" who aimed "to introduce Christianity to Christendom" face up to imitation. He confided to a Jewish friend, "With God the Father I could get along easier than with the Son, for He is the example that must be followed." Once introduced, the concept becomes the basis of his understanding of Christianity. (1) Imitation versus admiration: "Present-day Christians really live as though the position were that Christ was the great hero and benefactor who once and for all had secured happiness for us, and we only had to enjoy the innocent pleasures of the world and let him do the rest. But Christ is essentially the model, and consequently we should be *like* him and not merely make use of him." (2) The rebuke of imitation: "In relation to God's grace the insistence alters everything, reveals man's impotence before God, and drives him to Christ for mercy." (3) The grace accompanying imitation: "The 'imitation' must not, as Luther so admirably says, either hurl him into despair or presumption. If that moment comes (when *imitatio Christi* is welcomed), then in spite of all the suffering it brings the imitation is a thing of love, and so blessed." (4) Reduplication of the life of Christ: The first chapter of his book *The Gospel of Suffering* is entitled "The Joy that Lies in the Thought of Following Christ," and reads in part: "To follow Christ, then, means denying one's self, and hence it means walking the same way as Christ walked in the humble form of a servant—needy, forsaken, mocked, not loving worldliness and not loved by the worldly minded. Consequently, it means to walk alone . . ."

With all the Kierkegaardian peculiarity, nowhere does one find a better balance, *sacramentum et exemplum*. No Christian can escape imitation, but the secret lies in the Paradox-Pattern: "The true imitation is not produced by preaching on the theme: Thou shalt imitate Christ; but as a result of preaching about how much Christ has done for me. If a man grasps and feels that truly and profoundly then the imitation will follow naturally."

O Lord Jesus Christ, it was not to plague us men but to save us that Thou didst say, 'No man can serve two masters'—oh, that we might be willing to accept it, by doing it, that is, by following Thee! Help us all and everyone, Thou who art both willing and able to help, Thou who art both the Pattern and the Redeemer, and again both the Redeemer and the Pattern, so that when the striver sinks under the Pattern, then the Redeemer raises him up again, but at the same instant Thou art the Pattern, to keep him continually striving. Thou, our Redeemer, by Thy blessed suffering and death, hast made satisfaction for all and for everything; no eternal blessedness can be or shall be earned by desert—it has been deserved. Yet Thou didst leave behind Thee the trace of Thy footsteps, Thou the holy pattern of the human race and of each individual in it, so that, saved by Thy redemption, they might every instant have confidence and boldness to will to strive to follow Thee.

* * * * * *

'Imitation,' 'the following of Christ,' this precisely is the point where the human race winces, here it is principally that the difficulty lies, here is where the question really is decided whether one will accept Christianity or not. If pressure is brought to bear at this point, and a strong pressure—in that same degree there are few Christians. If at this point a convenient accommodation is made (so that Christianity becomes, intellectually, a doctrine), many enter into Christianity. If it is done away with entirely (so that Christianity becomes, existentially, as easy as mythology and poetry, while imitation is exaggeration, a ludicrous exaggeration), then Christianity widens out to such a degree that Christendom and the world almost correspond, or all become Christians, then Christianity has triumphed completely—in other words, it is done away with.

*   *   *   *   *   *

And so in the end one becomes tired of Christianity; for the pressure of imitation was lacking, the ideal, Christ as Pattern.

*   *   *   *   *   *

'Imitation,' which answers to 'Christ as the Pattern,' must be brought to the fore, applied, recalled to remembrance.

Let us take up the matter fundamentally, yet with all brevity. The Saviour of the world, our Lord Jesus Christ, did not come to the world to bring a doctrine; He never lectured. Since He did not bring a doctrine, neither did He seek to prevail upon anyone by reasons to accept the doctrine, nor seek with proofs to substantiate it. His teaching in fact was His life, His presence among men. If anyone desired to be His disciple, His way of going about it, as can be seen from the Gospel, was quite another way than the method of lecturing. He said to such a man something like this: 'Adventure a decisive action, then we can begin.' What does that mean? It means that one does not become a Christian by hearing something about Christ, by reading something, by thinking thereupon, or while Christ still lived upon earth, by seeing Him once in a while, or by going and gaping at Him the whole day. No, what is required is a *predicament (situation)*: adventure upon a decisive action, so that thou dost become heterogeneous with the life of this world, unable any longer to have thy life in it, dost find thyself in conflict with it—then thou wilt gradually be brought into such a tension that thou wilt be able to be observant of what I am here saying (says Christ). Perhaps also the tension will so affect thee that thou wilt understand that thou canst not support it without having recourse to Me, and so we can begin.

* * * * * *

Now it is well enough known that Christ constantly uses the expression "follower"; He never says anything about wanting admirers, admiring worshipers, adherents; and when he uses the expression "disciples," He always so explains it that we can perceive that followers are meant, that they are not adherents of a doctrine but followers of a life.

* * * * * *

We see therefore why Christ was born and lived in humiliation; no man, absolutely no man contemporary with him lived in such humiliation, there never lived a man so humiliated, and therefore it was absolutely impossible for any man to shirk the claims made upon him with the excuse or evasion that "the Pattern" was in possession of earthly and worldly advantages which he had not. In His actual life there was absolutely nothing to admire in that sense, unless one would admire poverty, wretchedness, the suffering of contempt, etc.

And in the situation of contemporaneousness there was not the least occasion to admire; for Christ had only the same conditions to offer to the man who would join Him, and on those conditions there was never any admirer who would take part. The same conditions: to become just as poor, as despised, as much scorned and mocked, and if possible even a little more.

What, then, is the distinction between "an admirer" and "a follower"? A follower is or strives *to be* what he admires; an admirer holds himself personally aloof, consciously or unconsciously, he does not discern that the object of his admiration makes a claim upon him to be or to strive to be the thing he admires.

So the distinction holds good nevertheless: the admirer is not willing to make any sacrifices, to give up anything worldly, to reconstruct his life, to be what he admires or let his life express it—but in words, verbal expressions, asseverations, he is inexhaustible in affirming how highly he prizes Christianity. The follower, on the other hand, aspires to be what he admires—and so (strange to say!) even though he lives in established Christendom he will encounter the same danger which once was involved in confessing Christ. Only the "followers" are the true Christians.

* * * * * *

No, the Pattern must be brought to the fore, for the sake at least of creating some respect for Christianity, to get it made a little bit evident what it is to be a Christian, to get Christianity transferred from learned discussion and doubt and twaddle (the objective) into the subjective sphere, where it belongs, as surely as the Saviour of the world, our Lord Jesus Christ, brought no doctrine into the world and never lectured but as the 'Pattern' required imitation—casting out, however, if possible, by His atonement all anxious dread from men's souls.

ANDREW MURRAY
[1828–1917]

"There are two classes of preachers that in our day claim
to be evangelical. Some are so eager to make disciples that
they do not hesitate to receive as such anyone professing;
others again act on the principle that the only way in which
anyone can become a genuine disciple is to exercise a
divinely-given faith in the example of the crucified Son of
God. It is to this latter class that Mr. Murray belongs."
So wrote a contemporary about the popular missionary-
evangelist who ranks along with Spurgeon, Moody, and
Truett.

The main part of his endeavors was spent in South Africa
in connection with the Dutch Reformed Church, but he
lectured widely throughout the world on missionary, Biblical,
and devotional subjects. He was popular among students,
and in this country appeared in Northfield and "Y" conferences. The bulk of his more than two dozen books were
mainly helps to devotion, and for this reason he has been
called "the Ignatius of modern evangelicals." His "With
Christ" series, in which the book *Like Christ* appears, had
a wide sale and can be found in almost any religious library; in fact, these works and others are still in print.

He confessed to being repetitious in his message. "Our
one need is, to know Jesus better" was his theme. He tried
hard, and exceedingly effectively, to keep evangelism harnessed for the practical life and the daily vocations. The
central thought of his largest work, *The Holiest of All*, an
exposition of the Epistle to the Hebrews, was, "Let us run
the race with patience, looking to Jesus." As the following
excerpts indicate, he was able to draw the fine distinction

163

between the redemptive element in the Cross and the responsive element in our cross-bearing. An incisive comment he often repeated called attention to the fact that Jesus said, "Follow me" when He was on earth, and "Abide in me" on going to heaven.

In all He suffered for us, He left us an example that we should follow in His footsteps. As the banner of the cross is lifted high, *the atonement of the cross* and *the fellowship of the cross* must equally be preached as the condition of true discipleship.

It is remarkable how distinctly this comes out in the teaching of the blessed Master Himself. In fact, in speaking of the cross, He gives its fellowship more prominence than its atonement. How often He told the disciples that they must bear it with Him and like Him; only thus could they be disciples, and share in the blessings His cross-bearing was to win. . . .

Christians need to understand that bearing the cross does not in the first place refer to the trials which we call crosses, but to that daily giving up of life, of dying to self, which must mark us as much as it did Jesus, which we need in times of prosperity almost more than in adversity, and without which the fulness of the blessing of the cross cannot be disclosed to us. It is the cross, not only as exhibited on Calvary, but as gloried in on account of its crucifying us, its spirit breathing through all our life and actions, that will be to the Christian and the Church as it was to Christ, the path to victory and to glory, the power of God for the salvation of men.

The Redemption of the cross consists of two parts—Christ

bearing the cross, Christ's crucifixion for us, as our atonement, the opening up of the way of life; our crucifixion, our bearing the cross with Christ, as our sanctification, our walking in the path of conformity to His blessed likeness. Christ the Surety and Christ the Example must equally be preached. . . .

The preacher who desires in this matter to lead his people in the path of entire conformity to the Saviour's likeness, will find a very wide field indeed opened up to him. The Christlike life is like a tree, in which we distinguish the *fruit*, the *root*, and the *stem* that connects the two. As in individual effort, so in the public ministry, THE FRUIT will probably first attract attention. The words of Christ, "Do ye even as I have done," and the frequent exhortations in the Epistles to love, and forgive, and forbear, even as Christ did, lead first to a comparison of the actual life of Christians with His, and to the unfolding and setting up of that only rule and standard of conduct which the Saviour's example is meant to supply. The need will be awakened of taking time and looking distinctly at each of the traits of that wonderful Portrait, so that some clear and exact impressions be obtained from it of what God actually would have us be. Believers must be brought to feel that the life of Christ is in very deed the law of their life, and that complete conformity to His example is what God expects of them. There may be a difference in measure between the sun shining in the heavens and a lamp lighting our home here on earth; still the light is the same in its nature, and in its little sphere the lamp may be doing its work as beautifully as the sun itself. The conscience of the Church must be educated to understand that the humility and self-denial of Jesus, His entire devotion to His Father's work and will, His ready obedience, His self-sacrificing love and kindly beneficence are nothing more than what each believer is to consider it his simple duty as well as his privilege to exhibit too. There is not, as so many think, one standard for Christ and another for His people. No; as branches of the vine, as members of the body, as partakers of the same spirit, we may and therefore must bear the image of the Elder Brother.

*   *   *   *   *   *

There is a twofold need of this lesson. With some there is the earnest desire and effort to follow Christ's example, without any sense of the impossibility of doing so, except by deep, real abiding in Him. They fail because they seek to obey the high command to live like Christ, without the only power that can do so—the living in Christ. With others there is the opposite error; they know their own weakness, and count the walking like Christ an impossibility. As much as those who seek to do it and who fail, do those who do not seek because they expect to fail, need the lesson we are enforcing. To walk like Christ one must abide in Him; he that abides in Him has the power to walk like Him; not indeed in himself or his own efforts, but in Jesus, who perfects His strength in our weakness. It is just when I feel my utter impotence most deeply, and fully accept Jesus in His wondrous union to myself as my life, that His power works in me, and I am able to lead a life completely beyond what my power could obtain. I begin to see that abiding in Him is not a matter of moments or special seasons, but the deep life process in which, by His keeping grace, I continue without a moment's intermission, and from which I act out all my Christian life. And I feel emboldened really to take Him in everything as my example, because I am sure that the hidden inner union and likeness must work itself out into a visible likeness in walk and conduct.

Only there is one thing I must not forget. It is not the remembrance of what Jesus has once done to me, but the living experience of what He is now to me, that will give me the power to act like Him. His love must be a present reality, the inflowing of a life and a power in which I can love like Him. It is only as by the Holy Spirit I realize WHAT Jesus is doing for me, and HOW He does it, and that it is HE who does it, that it is possible for me to do to others what He is doing to me.

* * * * * *

There is nothing that weakens the power of Christ's Example so much as the thought that we cannot really walk like Him. Do not listen to such thoughts. The perfect likeness in heaven is begun on earth, can grow with each day, and become more visible as life goes on. As certain and mighty as the work of surety which Christ, your Head, completed once for all, is the renewal after His own Image, which He is still working out. Let this double blessing make the cross doubly precious: Our Head suffered as a Surety, that in union with us He might bear sin for us. Our Head suffered as an Example, that He might show us what the path is in which, in union with Himself, He would lead us to victory and to glory. The suffering Christ is our Head, our Surety, and our Example.

And so the great lesson I have to learn is the wonderful truth that it is just in that mysterious path of suffering, in which He wrought out our atonement and redemption, that we are to follow His footsteps, and that the full experience of that redemption depends upon the personal fellowship in that suffering. "Christ suffered for us, leaving us an Example." May the Holy Spirit reveal to me what this means. . . .

Forgive me this, dear Lord, and teach me to find my happiness in union with Thee, my Head, not more in Thy Suretyship than in Thine Example. And grant, that in my meditations as to how I am to follow Thee, my faith may become stronger and brighter: Jesus is my Example because He is my life. I must and can be like Him, because I am one with Him. Grant this, my blessed Lord, for Thy love's sake.

Amen.

CHARLES SHELDON

[1857–1946]

GLENN CLARK

[1882–   ]

Fifty years separate Sheldon's best seller *In His Steps* (1896) and Clark's *What Would Jesus Do?*, but the latter is little more than an adaptation of the original theme to current problems. As Clark himself admitted, "The chief characters in this book are the grandchildren of the chief characters in Dr. Sheldon's book. . . . The solution to these problems in both cases is found in the answer to the simple question, 'What Would Jesus Do?' " The excerpts are accordingly taken from Dr. Clark's contemporary American version of the imitation theme which has been so popular among lay Christians.

For both books the Christ-way is the avenue out of our present dilemma; however, Clark's pays more attention to the primacy of the economic dilemma and the world at war. Both see in the life of Jesus the simple answer to our troubles. If only Christians would live like Christ in their daily vocations and interpersonal relations, and if the absolute love ethic exemplified by Jesus and codified in the Sermon on the Mount were unhesitantly copied in the life of every living Christian, the Kingdom of God would be ushered in throughout the world.

The expected ease with which this is to be accomplished is apparent in the second novel where the granddaughter Frances suggests to young paster Maxwell: "You know, I think our grandfather had the answer. Grandmother Rachel has told me about his wonderful experiment in living which began when he challenged his congregation with the question, 'What Would Jesus Do?' and actually tried following in his foot-

steps, every day, every hour. It was so thrilling to hear her
tell it. But there's the answer to everything, really. If only
we would question ourselves, 'What would Jesus do?' and
then try to follow through with the answer, we wouldn't
get into nearly so much trouble in our lives."

"Fifty years ago in this church, my grandfather conceived
a dream. From this pulpit he threw out a challenge. This
week I found in a cubbyhole in my grandfather's old desk a
copy of that sermon, and I shall at this time read to you a
portion of it."

Some of the older members of the audience sat alert at this
mention of Maxwell's revered predecessor.

" 'What I am going to propose now,' runs my grandfather's
words, 'is something which ought not to appear unusual or at
all impossible of execution. Yet I am aware that it will be so
regarded by a large number, perhaps, of the members of this
church. But in order that we may have a thorough understanding of what we are considering, I will put my proposition very plainly, perhaps bluntly. I want volunteers from the
First Church who will pledge themselves, earnestly and
honestly for an entire year, not to do anything without first
asking the question, What Would Jesus Do? And after asking
that question, each one will follow Jesus as exactly as he
knows how, no matter what the result may be. I will, of
course, include myself in this company of volunteers, and
shall take it for granted that my church here will not be
surprised at my future conduct, as based upon this standard
of action, and will not oppose whatever is done if they think
Christ would do it. Have I made my meaning clear? Our
motto will be, What Would Jesus Do? Our aim will be to
act just as He would if He were in our places, regardless of
immediate results. In other words, we propose to follow Jesus'

steps as closely and as literally as we believe He taught His disciples to do. And those who volunteer to do this will pledge themselves for an entire year, beginning with today, so to act.' "

Charles Maxwell placed the paper on the pulpit and looked genially over the audience. "I saw smiles of recognition on some of your faces as I read those words. Yes, it was an interesting experiment. For several years it did great things for our town. You probably all know some of your older friends and relatives who accepted the pledge. But this is a challenge that cannot be offered lightly and cannot be taken up without great sincerity, tremendous zeal, and a considerable amount of courage. What Would Jesus Do? has been the subject of many sermons since my grandfather's day, in this pulpit and all over the country. It has rarely been taken to heart. My new friends," he said, gently and firmly, "I think you have the courage and this is the crisis."

The skeptical faces scattered throughout the congregation had assumed blank looks, having been faced with a proposition which they could not, in all decency, dispute—not publicly, at least. And as the sense of peace and power continued within him, Charles saw that most of his people sat alert and interested. In a friendly, welcoming voice, he continued, "I am going to ask all those who want to take this pledge to meet with me at a special service tonight in the little chapel. There we can talk this thing over in detail, and map out this adventurous journey into real living. We shall try to follow Jesus as completely and literally as possible, regardless of the immediate results."

He left the pulpit and came out to the very edge of the platform. "Jesus was the only perfectly natural person who ever walked this earth. He followed laws of love as faithfully as the sea follows the laws of the tides. We as individuals and as nations have been living unnaturally. We have been breaking laws. This terrible war from which we are just emerging was the inevitable consequence of impractical, unnatural ways of living. If we persist in remaining out on the lunatic fringe of this revolving world we shall sooner or later all fall into the ditch.". . .

Before Charles had time to call on another, a veritable stream of words came pouring through the walrus mustaches of a lean, elderly man on the front seat.

"See here, young man," he said, not rising. He tossed his shaggy locks of grey hair and clenched his two bony hands around the top of the cane they held. "While you're talking about what Jesus would do, don't forget how He overturned the tables of the money-changers. We've got to put teeth in this if we get anywhere. The demon that is destroying America is greed, old demon greed. . . ."

And now the booming voice went on, "Does Editor Norman really want to do what Jesus would do? Does he really have the intestinal fortitude to knock over the money-changers' tables? Then the first thing he will do will be to remove the iron curtain that is hanging over our own news channels almost as tightly as it is hanging over Russia. He will have to lay bare the way our oil interests and other greedy monopolies are reaching out over the whole world in ways that may involve us in a new war almost before this one is ended."

"This is absurd!" exclaimed the bald-headed man sitting beside the speaker. "Now you are going too far, Babcock."

"Too far nothing," the deep bass boomed, and with one hand on his cane and the other on the chair, Babcock slowly rose to his feet and faced the audience.

"I am a pacifist, and I'll tell you why. Fifty years ago I took the pledge under my friend Henry Maxwell to walk in Jesus' steps."

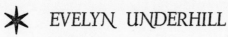

EVELYN UNDERHILL

[1875–1941]

The last message of Evelyn Underhill was a letter to one of her cherished prayer groups, this particular group being twelve young laywomen who called themselves "The Theological Kindergarten." It read in part: "Christianity can never be merely a pleasant or consoling religion. It is a stern business. It is concerned with the salvation through sacrifice and love of a world in which as we can all see now, evil and cruelty are rampant. Its supreme symbol is the Crucifix— the total and loving self-giving of man to the redeeming purposes of God."

This motif, the Crucifix as the perpetual sacrifice, the Pattern of all perfection, was for her the essence of Christian instruction and practice. Best of all she embodied it in her own brilliant career as teacher, counselor, author, humanitarian, and mystic. As for the last, well known is the fact that she was not only a first-rate historian of mysticism, but also perhaps our century's best-known Christian mystic. Her movement from general mysticism to avowedly Christian mysticism well within the bounds of the organized Church (she became an Anglican), is marked by her classics, from *Mysticism* (1911) to *Worship* (1936). Something happened to her during the early twenties, as she became more and more Christocentric, under the influence of the great and generous Catholic mystic, the Baron von Hügel.

But always her concerns were directed toward the active ministry in behalf of the needy. She, in her own words, was "only trying to be a decent third housemaid!" As one commentator puts it, "She really practised Ruysbroeck's 'widespreading love to all in common.'" For years she visited in the slums near her home twice a week and ministered to the poor. Her chief delight and occupation, besides being a housewife (married to lawyer H. Stuart Moore) and a scholar (the first woman lecturer at Oxford), was her yearly series of retreats, at which she excelled. A retreat for her was what one of the mystics called "a rest most busy." At these she never tired of offering the life of Christ as the pattern for self-development and self-offering.

When the Christian looks at the Crucifix, he looks at that which is for him the Pattern of all perfection . . . So, to be a member of the Church means not merely conformity to an institution, but incorporation in that living organism which only exists to express the Thought of God. It means becoming part of that perpetual sacrifice which continues in space and time the life of Incarnate Charity.

*   *   *   *   *   *

Now in each blade
I, blind no longer, see
The glory of God's growth: know it to be
An earnest of the Immemorial Plan.
Yea, I have understood
How all things are one great oblation made:
He on our altars, we on the world's rood.
Even as this corn,
Earth-born,
We are snatched from the sod;
Reaped, ground to grist,
Crushed and tormented in the Mills of God,
And offered at Life's hands, a living Eucharist.

*   *   *   *   *   *

The fully Christian life is a Eucharistic life: that is, a natural life conformed to the pattern of Jesus, given in its wholeness to God, laid on His altar as a sacrifice of love, and consequently transformed by His inpouring life, to be used to give life and food to other souls. It will be according to its measure and special call, adoring, declaratory, intercessory and redemptive: but always a vehicle of the Supernatural. The creative spirit of God is a redemptive and cherishing love; and it is as friends and fellow-workers with the Spirit, tools of the Divine redemptive action, that Christians are required to live.

* * * * * *

Must I be wounded in the busy hands
That labour to fulfil
Industrious love's demands
Within the circle of thy sovereign will?
And can it fall within that will to let
Thy child from all repayment of its debt?
   Yea, this must be
   If thou would'st work for Me:
   Thus only can
   My seal be set on man.

* * * * * *

All this suggests that though this outer discipline is very important for us, there is something deeper and more secret that God asks of us, if we really desire to give our lives to Him. Our Lord demanded great renunciation of those who wanted to follow Him. He never suggested that the Christian life was an easy or comfortable affair. The substance of what He asked is summed up in what are called the "evangelical counsels"—Poverty, Chastity and Obedience. We know that those who enter religious communities accept these counsels in their most literal form. They do give up all their posses-

sions, their natural and human relationships, the freedom of
their wills. But in one way or another, something of their
spirit is needed by everyone who really desires to follow
Christ. The New Testament means what it says when it
demands poverty of spirit, purity of heart and filial obedience
from all who would do this. . . .

First, think of *Poverty*. Even outward Poverty, a hard and
simple life, the dropping for love's sake of the many things
we feel we "must have" is a great help in the way of the
Spirit. Far more precious is that inward Poverty of which it
is the sacrament; which frees us from possessions and posses-
siveness and does away with the clutch of "the I, the Me
and the Mine" upon our souls. . . .

Chastity. The counsel of Chastity does not, of course,
mean giving up marriage but something much more subtle
and penetrating. It really means the spirit of poverty applied
to our emotional life—all the clutch and feverishness of
desire, the "I want" and "I must have" taken away and re-
placed by absolute single-mindedness, purity of heart. . . .
Christ's spirit of chaste Love will set us free; for it is a selfless,
all-embracing charity—friendship with God, and with all
His creatures for His sake. . . .

Obedience. This means the total surrender of our wills,
which are the great obstacles to our real self-giving to God.
The more we get rid of self-chosen aims, however good, the
more supple we are to His pressure, the nearer we get to the
pattern of the Christian life . . ."

*   *   *   *   *   *

He is disclosed both as Saviour and Pattern, especially to
those called to the service of Christ. . . . The more enrapt and
deliberate our contemplation of the window, the more our
little pretensions to Christianity shrink. There is God's
pattern for humanity and here am I. Lord, I am carnal, sold

under sin. Nevertheless I come here. I am a bit of your raw material, nothing more. I am to submit and re-submit to your teaching, healing, transfiguring action in order that I may be more useful to your other children. That is what matters. In some way or other each of your states and mysteries concerns my soul and my prayer. I am to think of that. Perhaps in the silence I shall understand it better than before.

✳ DIETRICH BONHOEFFER
[1906–1945]

This modern Christian saint presented the imitation of Christ appropriately: theory before practice. His book *The Cost of Discipleship* appeared first under the German title *Nachfolge Christi* in 1937. On April 9, 1945, Bonhoeffer met his death at the hands of Hitler's Black Guards, thus carrying his Christian loyalty to the actual point of taking up his cross and going to his own Golgotha. He simply exhibited what he and the foregoing authors specified as the heart of Christianity—the imitation of Christ. "Throughout the Christian life, from baptism to martydom, it is the same suffering and the same death." How ominous were his words!

In his theory he exposed "cheap grace"; in his life he exhibited "costly grace." "Such grace is *costly* because it calls us to follow, and it is *grace* because it calls us to follow Jesus Christ." He insisted that true discipleship is followship: "The only man who has the right to say that he is justified by grace alone is the man who has left all to follow Christ." "So the disciple is a disciple only in so far as he shares his Lord's suffering and rejection and crucifixion."

Facing the "impossible ethic" of the Sermon on the Mount, as he had learned to call it under his Neo-orthodox teachers, he did not try to hedge or rationalize; rather he sought every means by which to re-incarnate it. Where others have tried frantically to escape the stringent demands of the love-ethic, having just enough religion to make them uneasy, Bonhoeffer in his writings and in his death appears to have followed Christ so absolutely as to possess the peace that passeth understanding.

"Whom he foreknew, he also foreordained to be conformed to the image of his Son, that he might be the firstborn among many brethren" (Rom. viii.29). Here is a promise which passes all understanding. Those who follow Christ are destined to bear His image, and to be the brethren of the firstborn Son of God. Their goal is to become "as Christ." Christ's followers always have His image before their eyes, and in its light all other images are screened from their sight. It penetrates into the depths of their being, fills them and transforms them, and makes them copies of their Master. Such is the effect of daily fellowship and communion with Christ. No follower of Jesus can contemplate His image in a spirit of cold detachment. That image has the power to transform our lives, and if we surrender ourselves utterly to Him, we cannot help bearing His image ourselves. We become the sons of God, we stand side by side with Christ, our unseen Brother, bearing like Him the image of God. . . .

An image needs a living object, and a copy can only be formed from a model. Either man models himself on the god of his own invention, or the true and living God moulds the human form into His image. There must be a complete transformation, a "metamorphosis" (Rom. xii.2; 2 Cor. iii.18), if man is to be restored to the image of God. How then is that transformation to be effected? . . .

God sends His Son—here lies the only remedy. It is not enough to give man a new philosophy or a better religion. A Man comes to men. Every man bears an image. His body and his life become visible. A man is not a bare word, a thought or a will. He is above all and always a man, a form, an image, a brother. Hence if he is to become a new creature he must acquire not only a new mental outlook, not only a new direction of will or a new pattern of behaviour, but a new image and a new form. Now in Jesus Christ this is just what has happened. The image of God has entered our midst, in the form of our fallen life, in the likeness of sinful flesh. In the teaching and acts of Christ, in His life and death, the image of God is revealed. In Him the divine image has been recreated on earth. The Incarnation, the words and acts of Jesus, His death on the cross, are all indispensable parts of that image. But it is not the same image as Adam bore in the primal glory of paradise. Rather, it is the image of one who enters a world of sin and death, who takes upon Himself all the sorrows of humanity, who meekly bears God's wrath and judgement against sinners, and obeys His will with unswerving devotion in suffering and death, the Man born to poverty, the friend of publicans and sinners, the Man of sorrows, rejected of man and forsaken of God. Here is God made man, here is man in the new image of God.

We know full well that the marks of the passion, the wounds of the cross, are now become the marks of grace in the Body of the risen and glorified Christ.

* * * * * *

There is always a danger that in our asceticism we shall be tempted to imitate the sufferings of Christ. This is a pious but godless ambition, for beneath it there always lurks the notion that it is possible for us to step into Christ's shoes and suffer as He did. We are then presuming to undertake that bitter work of eternal redemption which Christ Himself wrought for us. The motive of asceticism was more limited— to equip us for better service and deeper humiliation. But it can only do that so long as it takes the suffering of Christ as its basis; if not, it degenerates into a dreadful parody of the Lord's own passion.

*   *   *   *   *   *

To be conformed to the image of Christ is not an ideal to be striven after. It is not as though we had to imitate Him as well as we could. We cannot transform ourselves into His image, it is rather the form of Christ which seeks to be formed in us (Gal. iv.19), and to be manifested in us. Christ's work in us is not finished until He has perfected His own form in us. We must be assimilated to the form of Christ in its entirety, the form of Christ incarnate, crucified and glorified.

*   *   *   *   *   *

But if we behold Jesus Christ going on before step by step, if we only look to Him and follow Him, step by step, we shall not go astray. But if we worry about the dangers that beset us, if we gaze at the road instead of at Him who goes before, we are already straying from the path. For He is Himself the way, the narrow way and the strait gate. He, and He alone, is our journey's end.

*   *   *   *   *   *

The Holy Trinity Himself has made His dwelling in the Christian heart, filling his whole being, and transforming him into the divine image. Christ, incarnate, crucified and glorified is formed in every Christian soul, for all are members of His Body, the Church. The Church bears the human form, the form of Christ in His death and resurrection. The Church in the first place is His image, and through the Church each several member. In the Body of Christ we are become "like Christ."

Now we can understand why the New Testament always speaks of our becoming "like Christ." We have been transformed into the image of Christ, and are therefore destined to be like Him. He is the only "pattern" we must follow.

And because He really lives His life in us, we too can "walk even as he walked" (1 John ii.6), and "do as he has done" (John xiii.15), "love as he has loved" (Eph. v.2; John xiii.34, xv.12), "forgive as he forgave" (Col. iii.13), "have this mind, which was also in Christ Jesus" (Phil. ii.5), and therefore we are able to follow the example He has left us (1 Pet. ii.21), lay down our lives for the brethren as He did (1 John iii.16). It is only because He became like us that we can become like Him. It is only because we are identified with Him that we can become like Him. By being transformed into His image, we are enabled to model our lives on His. By simply following Him we can perform deeds and live a life which is one with the life of Christ. We are now able to render spontaneous obedience to the word of God. We no longer regard our own lives or the new image which we bear, for then we should at once have forfeited it. No, we must look steadfastly on the reflection of the image of Jesus Christ. The disciple looks solely at his Master. But when a man follows Jesus Christ and bears the image of the incarnate, crucified and risen Lord, when he has become the image of God, we may at last say that he has been called to be the "imitator of God." The follower of Jesus is the imitator of God. "Be ye therefore imitators of God, as beloved children" (Eph. v.1). . . .

A few, but only a few, of His followers are accounted worthy of the closest fellowship with His sufferings—the blessed martyrs. No other Christian is so closely identified with the form of Christ crucified. When Christians are exposed to public insult, when they suffer and die for His sake, Christ takes on visible form in His Church. Here we see the divine image created anew through the power of Christ crucified. But throughout the Christian life, from baptism to martyrdom, it is the same suffering and the same death.

✳ PHILIPPE VERNIER
[1909–   ]

Known as a "modern St. Francis," Philippe Vernier, living in France under the darkest clouds of war-torn, hate-mongering, and enslaved industrial society, has yet maintained the joyous, redemptive spirit of Christ. He has suffered deprivation in his life of service among the rough boys, miners, underprivileged, sick, and spiritually distraught. He has suffered the hardships of a mission field. He has even suffered disdain at the hands of church officials who would not sanction his all-out Christianity. But in facing all of these setbacks, his life has exhibited the spirit of those who have been "with the Master."

He has suffered most in his labors for peace. Like his Master he has devoted his life to reconciling people with people and the world with God. He has sought for peace in the lives of the villagers and miners with whom he comes into daily contact. (He pastors a Huguenot church in Mauberge.) For him this has meant primarily the outpouring of a loving spirit to all those with whom he has dealings, working in the mines so that he can know and help miners at firsthand, struggling always to replace the fear and self-centeredness in men's minds with the security and compassion that come from love. Perhaps in his firsthand association with the common people, the identification of the loving heart, he imitates Christ most.

His uncompromising efforts for peace among the nations have thrown him into prison for years, one time into solitary confinement for twenty-four months. His cell became an opportunity for companionship with God: "God was so near and real that I was sometimes almost overpowered," he confided. Growing from those experiences have come these meditations which, whether given as testimonies before courts, army and prison officials, or conveyed to the reader in the ease of a study or boudoir chair, challenge every soul to live *With the Master*—the title given to the series.

LET HIM TAKE UP HIS CROSS DAILY

LUKE 9:23

Of all the passages of the New Testament that we have devitalized and made insipid, few have been more abused than this. Frequently you will hear good people—a mother with a disobedient child, or a comrade whose work bores him —say, lifting eyes to heaven, "What a cross!" They really imagine that because a little nuisance bothers them from time to time they have "taken up their cross" and are "following him"!

Their crime is that they adapt the gospel to the humdrum of their lives; they drag Jesus down to their level, instead of admitting frankly that he demands too much of them.

One would offend the Master less by spurning his appeal outright than by thus saying to him: "See, I am obeying you! I walk in your steps. I, too, carry my cross!" That is mocking him.

When the Master said, "Let him take up his cross," he conjured up a precise image: the horrible and supreme humiliation of slaves condemned to death. In Rome the insult with which one lashed a slave was "crucifer," cross-bearer, as we might say "gallows bird." To explain to his disciples what "denying oneself" meant, and how far it should go, Jesus spoke of the worst outrages that could be inflicted on the lowest class of men.

"Denying oneself" means to be ready to descend to the last rung of the ladder, to become the object of general disdain, to die pitifully, shamefully, hearing those around one say: "Good riddance for society!"

That is what "following" the Master would be; that is what "taking up one's cross" would mean, and not our way of seasoning our unshaken lives with a bit of evangelical poetry.

We might as well know it: it is not at all easy to be a Christian.

*   *   *   *   *   *

THAT YE SHOULD FOLLOW HIS STEPS

I PETER 2:21

You would become the imitator of your Master? How can you even dream of it? Aside from the fact that he is the Son of God and you the least of sinners, that he is innocent of any fault while yours bar your way to Heaven, even if you wish to imitate only the externals of his life, it would be impossible for you to resemble him.

Would you seek to acquire his tone of authority, the air of sovereignty that makes him the Master? Then you would forget that he is also the one who, kneeling, washes the feet of his disciples.

Would you create for yourself the role of a prophet? Would you inveigh against the wealthy and the bigots? Would you gird yourself with the rough tunic of John the Baptist and preach repentance? You would not be at the same time the friend and the brother of all men, who willingly sits down at a wedding feast, takes children on his knees, gazes upon flowers in the fields.

Were you to try to concern yourself with the affairs of God and to cling to the world above, you would not, like him, know how to attend to the complaints of humble people, relieving their hurts and sharing their miseries.

For he is at the same time magnificent and modest, terrible and tender, of heaven and of earth, close to God and the companion of men. You yourself cannot be all this at once.

But then what does it mean to follow his steps? It is not literally imitating him, it is loving what he says, what he does, what he is; contemplating him often, filling your heart with his image. He himself will then show you how to follow him.

*   *   *   *   *   *

THOU CANST NOT FOLLOW ME

JOHN 13:36

The apostle you resemble most is Simon Peter. Like him you are made up of a little enthusiasm and a lot of cowardice; like him you confess your Master in impressive speeches, immediately afterwards to deny him before an ill-wisher or a mocker, hiding yourself in a corner when you should appear at his side.

You say you would give your life for him but then he reminds you that you are not capable of following him. You are too unsteady. You may have fine impulses, but that does not suffice to make you his disciple. The road he follows is long and hard, and he walks straight ahead on it, without mistaking the way, without drawing back, without hesitating.

In truth, you cannot follow him. Your own walk is a series of jerks: now you run, now you stop; today floating in highest heaven in jubilation at belonging to God, tomorrow in the depths of despair, in the resigned recognition of Satan's power.

How could you follow him? No one has been able to. An unexpected obstacle or a moment of inattention makes you lose the way. The Master is far off when you want to rejoin him. While you were losing your time in perpetual detours he was advancing along a straight line, firmly climbing his Calvary.

One hope remains to you, however. The Master said: "Thou canst not follow me now." That means that one day you will be able to, when he has cured you of your incoherence, and shaped you to his obedience. When he has filled you with his power, "afterwards"—soon perhaps!—you will follow him.

✳ SOURCES

Ignatius   *The Ante-Nicene Fathers*, Vol. I, pp. 50-51, 69, 75-76, 88. New York: Christian Literature Company, 1885, 1896.

Clement of Alexandria   *The Ante-Nicene Fathers*, Vol. II, Book I, Chapter XII, p. 234. New York: Christian Literature Company, 1885, 1896.

Cyprian   *The Ante-Nicene Fathers*, Vol. V, pp. 484-490. New York: Christian Literature Company, 1885, 1896.

Lactantius   *The Ante-Nicene Fathers*, Vol. VII, pp. 124-128. New York: Christian Literature Company, 1885, 1896.

Basil the Great   *The Ascetic Works of Saint Basil*, translated by W. K. L. Clarke, pp. 216, 130-131. London: Society for Promoting Christian Knowledge, 1925. Used by permission.

Augustine   "The Christian Combat," *The Fathers of the Church*, edited by Ludwig Schopp, Vol. 4, pp. 327-330. New York: CIMA Publishing Co., Inc., 1947.

Gregory the Great   *Morals on the Book of Job*, Vol. II, pp. 251, 524; Vol. III, pp. 412-413, 288. Oxford: John Henry Parker, 1844.

Bernard of Clairvaux   *The Steps of Humility*, translated by George Bosworth Burch, p. 123. Cambridge: Harvard University Press, 1940. Used by permission.
Cantica Canticorum, translated by Samuel J. Eales, pp. 289, 83-85, 269-270. London: Elliot Stock, 1895.

Francis of Assisi   *The Words of St. Francis*, compiled by James Meyer, pp. 9-11, 16, 250, 261, 274. Chicago: Franciscan Herald Press, 1952. Used by permission.

Thomas Aquinas   *The Summa Theologica*, as found in Great Books
of the Western World Series, Vol. 20, pp. 656-
657, 658, 659. Chicago: Encyclopaedia Britan-
nica, 1952. London: Burns, Oates & Washbourne. Used by permission. American rights
granted by Benziger Brothers, Inc., New York.
The Summa Theologica of St. Thomas Aquinas,
Vol. 16, Part III, QQ. XL, Arts. 1 & 2, pp.
191-192, 193. London: Burns, Oates & Washbourne, 1926. Used by permission. American
rights granted by Benziger Brothers, Inc., New
York.

David of   *Spiritual Life and Progress*, Vol. I, pp. 21-23, 74.
Augsburg   London: Burns, Oates & Washbourne, 1937.
Used by permission.

Meister Eckhart   *Meister Eckhart*, edited by Franz Pfeiffer, Vol.
I, p. 452; Vol. II, pp. 23-24; Vol. I, pp. 262-
263, 229. London: John Watkins, 1924. Para-
graphing altered.
The Works of Meister Eckhart, translated by
C. de B. Evans, Vol. II, pp. 95-96. London:
John Watkins, 1931.

Richard Rolle   *Selected Works of Richard Rolle*, transcribed by
G. C. Heseltine, p. 85. London: Longmans,
Green & Co. Ltd., 1930. Used by permission.
Late Medieval Mysticism, edited by Ray C. Petry,
p. 221. Published, 1957, The Westminster Press.
Used by permission.
A Book of the Love of Jesus, pp. 101-104. Lon-
don: Sir Isaac Pitman & Sons Ltd., 1904.

Henry Suso   *The Life of Blessed Henry Suso*, translated by
Thomas Francis Knox, pp. 1, 21-22, 50, 61-62,
149-150, 220. London: Burns, Lambert, and
Oates, 1865.

Theologia   *Theologia Germanica*, pp. 152-153, 203, 215-216,
Germanica   145, 159-161. New York: Pantheon Books, Inc.,
1949. Used by permission.

Ludolphus   *Vita*, Vol. III, Second Part, Ch. II, pp. 11-12.
Paris: Victorem Palme, 1878. (Selection translated from the Latin.)

Gerard Groote — *Meister Eckhart Und Die Devotion Moderna*, compiled and edited by Maria Lücker, p. 98. Leiden: E. J. Brill, 1950. Used by permission. (Selection translated from the German.)

Gerard Zerbolt — *The Imitation of Christ*, translated by Albert Hyma, pp. 74, 113-116. Grand Rapids: Wm. B. Eerdmans Publishing Co., 1950. Used by permission.

Thomas à Kempis — *The Imitation of Christ*. From *The Christian's Pattern*, John Wesley's translation of portions of *The Imitation of Christ*. Excerpts found within pp. 103-115. London: for John Rivington, 1750.

Erasmus — *A Sermon on the Child Jesus*, edited by J. H. Lupton, pp. 19, 21, 6, 12-13, 25-27. London: George Bell and Sons, 1901. Spelling modernized.

Martin Luther — *Saemtliche Schriften*, edited by J. Georg Walch, Vol. 9. St. Louis: Concordia Publishing House, 1893. Used by permission. (Selection translated from the German.)
"On the Councils and the Churches," *Works of Martin Luther*, Vol. V, p. 161. Philadelphia: Muhlenberg Press, 1931. Used by permission.

Ignatius Loyola — *The Spiritual Exercises*, translated by Fr. Elder Mullan, S. J., pp. 55-58, 73-76, 84. New York: P. J. Kenedy and Sons, 1914. Used by permission.

John Calvin — *The Institutes of the Christian Religion*, Vol. I, pp. 619, 620, 625, 629-630. Philadelphia: Presbyterian Board of Publications, 1813. John Allen edition (6th).

St. Teresa — *The Complete Works of Saint Teresa of Jesus*, translated and edited by E. Allison Peers from the critical edition of P. Silverio de Santa Teresa, C. D., Vol. II, pp. 304-305, 308; Vol. I, p. 139; Vol. II, pp. 366-367, 370, 382, 398-399; Vol. III, pp. 289, 299. Published in three volumes by Sheed and Ward, Inc., New York, 1946. Used by permission.

John Arndt — *Of True Christianity*, pp. xlvii, 495-496, 542-543, 499-500. London: Joseph Downing, 1720. Spelling modernized.

Jeremy Taylor   *The Great Exemplar of Sanctity and Holy Life*, Vol. I, pp. 68, 70-71, 73, 74-75, 77, 83, London: John Hatchard and Son, 1835.

James Nayler   *There Is a Spirit, The Nayler Sonnets*, Kenneth Boulding, p. x. New York: Fellowship Publications, 1945.

William Penn   *No Cross, No Crown*, pp. 22-23, 8, 36-38, 218-219. Philadelphia: Friends' Book Store, n.d.

François Fénelon   *Christian Perfection*, edited by Charles F. Whiston, pp. 43-44. New York: Harper & Brothers, 1947. Used by permission.

William Law   *A Practical Treatise upon Christian Perfection*, pp. 299-300, 302, 311, 314, 316, 320, 316. Portsmouth: Charles Morgridge, 1822. First American edition.

Charles Wesley   *Sacred Poetry*, selected from the works of Charles Wesley, pp. 429-430. New York: D. Appleton & Co., 1864.

Jonathan Edwards   *A Treatise on Religious Affections*, edited by W. Ellerby, pp. 33, 38, 204, 205-206, 239, 242, 273. New York: American Tract Society, n.d.

Ein Send-Brief   *Ein Send-Brief*, samt einem schonen Gebatt und geistlichen, pp. 77-79, 92-94. Leiden, 1715? (Selection translated from the German.)

Schleitheim Confession of Faith   *Great Voices of the Reformation*, edited by Harry Emerson Fosdick, pp. 291-292. New York: Random House, 1952.

John Woolman   *Journal*, pp. 189-191. New York: E.P. Dutton & Co., n.d. Used by permission.

Soren Kierkegaard   *For Self-Examination and Judge for Yourselves!*, pp. 197, 209, 200, 216-217, 161. Princeton: Princeton University Press, 1944. Used by permission.
Christian Ethics, edited by Waldo Beach and H. Richard Niebuhr, pp. 432, 436-437. New York: The Ronald Press, 1955.

Andrew Murray   *Like Christ*, pp. 226-231, 3-4, 10-11, 23-24. New York: J.H. Sears & Company, Inc., n.d.

Evelyn Underhill   From the book *An Anthology on the Love of God*, by Evelyn Underhill, pp. 81, 88, 90, 27. Published by E.P. Dutton & Co., Inc. and reprinted with their permission. London: A.R. Mowbray & Co., 1953. Used by permission of Messrs. Longmans, Green & Co. Ltd. for the extracts from *The School of Charity* and *The Mystery of Sacrifice* by Evelyn Underhill.
The Fruits of the Spirit, pp. 65-68. London: Longmans, Green & Co. Ltd., 1942. Used by permission.
Light of Christ, pp. 33-35. London: Longmans, Green & Co. Ltd., 1945. Used by permission.

Glenn Clark   *What Would Jesus Do?*, pp. 35-37, 42-44. St. Paul: Macalester Park Publishing Company, 1946. Used by permission.

Dietrich Bonhoeffer   *The Cost of Discipleship*, pp. 192, 193, 194, 148, 195, 163, 197-198, 196. New York: The Macmillan Company, 1949. Used by permission.

Philippe Vernier   *With the Master*, pp. 32, 45, 48. Nyack, New York: Fellowship Publications, 1943. Used by permission.